Headmasterji

Headmasterji

The Man with Literacy Mission

SANDEEP SHARMA

PARTRIDGE
A Penguin Random House Company

ISBN:	Softcover	978-1-4828-5764-1
	eBook	978-1-4828-5763-4

Print information available on the last page.

To order additional copies of this book, contact
Partridge India
000 800 10062 62
orders.india@partridgepublishing.com

www.partridgepublishing.com/india

Contents

Acknowledgement

Its three years back the journey to know Headmasterji of Surajgarh, the first educated man – the first official graduate in 1932 and postgraduate in 1936 in the history of Surajgarh in the era before independence in 1947. When I picked up the subject and wrote a biographical sketch of Rambilas Sharma and the education upliftment of Surajgarh, most of the people in the family, friends, relatives were not in favour of it. But I firmly decided to go ahead on it, as I, myself, wanted to pay tribute to my legendary grandfather-the man behind the literacy mission for Surajgarh.

I must remember and thank all those people who were so positive in providing me the information about Rambilas Sharma- who have directly or indirectly helped me in this effort to pay my tribute to the man who made a history in educational map of Surajgarh, rather the Tall building of education today stands on the foundation stone named –Rambilas Sharma-Headmasterji.-Guruji for thousands of thousands – chachaji for few – dadaji for few more.

I had decided to fetch details about a person who died almost four decades ago. I came across many who brought excuses and did not provide any details, though they know their life was guided by Headmasterji.

But there has been a positive group of people who wanted that this happen. I am thankful to all of them. My inspiration has been my grandfather himself. But the positive force in my life my son Navya Sharma who often says that "papa I will make a book on your and dadu's life." I am glad about his positive gesture. My thanks to my mother Smt. Sita Sharma and especially my father Savitaprakash Sharma who wanted me to finish this book as soon as possible.

I am thankful to Godawaridevi –Headmasterji's sister, who provided me vital information about Headmasterji;s life, early age, about the family. Despite of being 95 yrs of age she had remarkable memory. I had conducted her interview, unfortunately she is no more to see the book, and she passed away in 2014.

I am thankful to all six children of Rambilasji Sharma- Omprakash Sharma, Satyaprakash Sharma, Savitaprakash Sharma, Gayatridevi, Sajjan kumar Sharma, Suniti kumar Sharma, for verifying the details ofcontent and adding missing details. I extend my thanks to my brother Sanjeev Sharma and sister Seema Sharma who would patiently listen to me and give their inputs. Besides that even my sister-in-law Reenu Sharma and kids of my family Navya, Daivya and Neetigya, who despite not knowing much about this work, would respect my effort.

I am thankful to Late. Matadin ji Khandelwal-station road, Surajgarh, who was student, colleague, and who supported headmasterji as a sixth son to Headmasterji, for the information given during the interviews conducted at Surajgarh.

I am thankful to Sewaram Gupta-Surajgarh for permitting me collect information from old records of photographs from PB high school Surajgarh, and Bhunesh gupta (son of Sewaramji Gupta)- my friend, and a rising potitician from Surajgarh, for personally accompanying me to PB High School to collect details and information. I must also thank all the staff members and principal for their cooperation in this task.

I am thankful to my friends from Surajgarh who have been actively commenting on headmasterji's Facebook page- including Arun kumar Pushkarna, Hiralalji joshi, Arvind Joshi, Naveen Agarwal(Late Babulalji's son), Murlidhar Badraika, Jugalkishore Chawla, Mahavirprasadji sharma, Late. Jugal Kishore Barasia(whom I met in his kalbadevi, Mumbai office in 1996-97), Jagdishprasad Tibrawal, Vedprakash Verma-Faridabad, omkarmal Agarwal(Surajgarh Mandi), Sunderlal Sharma-RPS, Chirawa, Chapparias from Surajgarh, Suresh Saini(Mount Abu) and D.K.Jangid.

I am also thankful to some people who negatively motivated me by not providing any information inspite of them having a handful of information.

I am thankful to Dr. Ekta Sharma-my wife, without whose constant support and help especially while working at the end of the book, for completing thebook. She has been motivating throughout the last 3 years. Many atimes my business work and personal work also suffered. But she extended her support throughout.

I am thankful to all people who directly or indirectly helped me to complete my task. Last but not the least, I am indebted to Lord Almighty, to give me an opportunity to know my grandfather and his humble work.

I love you and respect you Dadoji. And I love you Surajgarh.

Jai Shree Shyam

Preface

When I saw my son, Navya, going to temple with my father, Savita Prakash Sharma, I remembered my grandfather- Rambilasji Sharma "Headmasterji", taking me on his shoulder to nearby Hanuman temple.

Headmaster ji has gifted me (Sandeep- Grandson & author) a small alphabetical English book, which the author has preserved till date. It is an Educational Blessing from the man with the literacy mission.

Headmasterji's grandson, was the first among family kids to be photographed at the age of less than one year, as Headmasterji wanted to keep his grandson's photograph with him.

Rambilasji wished to name me(Author) as Peeyush, meaning nectar, but his wife Janaki Devi insisted that since Rambilas ji had always been the devotee of Lord Surya, which enlightens all lives, their grandson's name should have name which means illumination, enlightening the lives. So, he decided to christen his grandson "Sandeep". Whenever any family member takes the name of "Sandeep" they remember Headmasterji.

Headmaster ji- My Grandfather was attached to me. When I was merely two years old, anybody coming to meet my grandfather, would see me playing and my grandfather would tell them with proud that he is my grandson, Sandeep. He is very intelligent. Then he would call me and ask me to recite English poems, which I would also do readily and he would bless me. He would say," Issi tarah Padho aur aage badho." Today it is by his blessings that I could attain Higher & professional Education. The guests would be very glad that a boy of merely two years old, who is not going to school and can recite English poems so nicely, in year 1974-75, in a small village of merely population of 18 thousand people.

As a grandson, I used to enjoy a very special bond with my grandfather. I observed that he commanded lot of respect from the society. I had seen most of the people coming to meet him would bow down to touch his feet, to mark a respect to the towering personality, Headmasterji.

I have seen him working hard and not giving up & his life teaches me, "Suraj na ban paye to ban ke Deepak jalata chal, Phool mila ya angare, such ki rahon pe chalta chal". He lived these lines. He truly gave his life for the upliftment of people of Surajgarh.

He was the "Neev ki Eent"(foundation stone) for tall building of education in Surajgarh. I would ask (as a child) to headmasterji about his likings & dislikings & he would very politely only answer vcery specifically about the question.

I remember as a young kid of five years, about his last few minutes of life, he called his eldest son "Omprakash ji" and asked him to sit in "Tibari" and then Headmaster ji put his head in his son's lap and he poured drops of Gangajal in Headmasterji's mouth. And his other son was reciting Bhagwat Puran and his friend and Vaidya Sh. Madan Lal ji Pushkarna held headmasterji's hand, to test the nadi and he said, "Nadi nahin mil rahi. Doob rahi hai" and on that Headmasterji smiled and gave ashirwaad to all. I ran barefooted to the funeral ground crying and shouting "Where are you taking away my Dada ji?"

After his death whenever we visited my grandmother to Surajgarh, at the railway station, we would get down, Tonga Wala, would ask us, "Katthe jaano hai Bhaaiya(Where do you want to go)?" and my father always replied, "Headmasterji ke gharaain" (Headmasterji's house). Hearing this Tonga wala would immediately lift our luggage and would request all males to sit in front seat and give females privilege to occupy rear seat.

I feel proud that people remember him even after thirty six years of his death and this make me think," How could people remember somebody after 36 years of his death? What type of life did headmasterji lead? How do people love him even after his death?"

In 2012, the idea struck to pen down incidents of a life from a common man, whom common men of Surajgarh still remember after 36 years of his death.

And then begin an enjoyable journey to know headmasterji &Surajgarh. The data has been collected through interviewing Headmasterji's family, friends, students and colleagues.

About the Author

The author's full name is Sandeep Savitaprakash Sharma. Born at Surajgarh in 15-12-1973, and remained in Surajgarh for 5 yrs up to 1977 along with Rambilash Sharma- Headmasterji, who was the author's grand father.

The author did his schooling through out in conventand did B.Sc-electronics M.Sc- Electronics (From famous Bhavans college, Ahnedabad) and MBA-Marketing from Ahmedabad. Also pursued PGDCA-computers from St. Xaviers College, Ahmedabad.

After working for a German company for initially 6 years, startedhis own venture, and is now Director of Magnum Opus International-Ahmedabad. The author has written few technical articles in spectroscopy in the Jounal of Indian Foundry.

The author is passionate about Surajgarh and sees all positive things in his village.

Over and above technical background, the author is man behind rediscovering Rambilasji Sharma and Surajgarh. He made many contributions about Surajgarh on internet. He made Surajgarh popular on social media by forming the group- "I belong to Surajgarh" for bringing all from Surajgarh on one platform- globally. Today it is the largest groupabout Surajgarh on facebook having thousands of members from all over the globe. He has contributed about Surajgarh shekhawati on many blogs. He is founder president of International shekhawati cultural preservation foundation. The revenues generated from his books will be donated to such foundation for the developments of Surajgarh, shekhawati in Rajasthan, India.

Further he created many pages and blogs about Surajgarh, and all Surajgarhian have been loving it.

He has contributed thousands of photographs from Surajgarh on facebook, panorama, google, google plus, wiki pedia and many other …

This book is his first book, and he is already writing another one onSurajgarh.

The author is residing in Ahmedabad, India, for last 32 yrs.

Resume of Rambilasji Sharma-"Headmasterji"

NAME: RAMBILAS GAJANAND SHARMA

BIRTH: 13TH MAY 1913

DEATH: 07THNOVEMBER 1977

PLACE:SURAJGARH, DIST. JHUNJHUNU, RAJASTHAN, INDIA

Chart - 1: QUALIFICATION

SR.NO.	QUALIFICATIONS	GRADE	YEAR OF PASSING	INSTITUTE OF PASSING	PLACE
001	INITIAL BASIC VEDIC AND SANSKRIT EDUCATION	FIRST	1917	FROM GRANDFATHER FAMOUS PANDIT. LOKRAMJI GHAGSHYAN	**SURAJGARH**
002	MATRICULATION	FIRST	1927	MAHDEV SOMANY HIGH SCHOOL,	CHIRAWA
003	INTERMEDIATE	FIRST	1929	MAHDEV SOMANY HIGH SCHOOL	"
004	BACHELOR OF ARTS-ENGLISH	FIRST	1932	GOVERNMENT COLLEGE	Lahore
005	MASTER OF ARTS -ENGLISH	FIRST	1936	GOVERNMENT COLLEGE	Lahore
006	MASTER OF ARTS-HINDI	FIRST	1938	ALLAHABAD UNIVERSITY	AGRA
007	MASTER OF ARTS-SANSKRIT	FIRST	1954	ALLAHBAD UNIVERSITY	AGRA
008	BACHLOR OF EDUCATION	FIRST	1956	AGRA UNIVERSITY	AGRA
009	SAHITYA RATNA	FIRST	1957	Visharad -Hindi SahityaSammelan; Teacher, High Schools and Multipurpose HrSecSchools, 1956 Onwards;Member of Board of SecEdn, Rajasthan; Nationalisation Board OfTextBook, Rajasthan	Jaipur
010	AYURVED RATNA	FIRST	1961	ALLAHBAD UNIVERSITY	ALLAHBAD
011	YOGA ACHARYA	FIRST	1963	ALLAHBAD UNIVERSITY	ALLAHBAD
012	SAMAJ RATNA	FIRST	1971	SURAJGARH, DIST. JHUNJHUNU, RAJASTHAN	SUAJGARH
013	SHIKSHA RATNA		1971	JHUNJHUNU	RAJASTHAN

PROFESSIONAL JOURNEY:

Chart - 2: Work experience

SR NO.	INSTITUTE	POSITION	YEAR	PLACE
001	RAGHUVIR VIDHAYALAYA	TEACHER	1932-34	BISSAU
002	CHIRAWA HIGH SCHOOL	TEACHER	1936-41	CHIRAWA
003	BIRLA HIGH SCHOOL	PRINCIPAL	1941-43	OKARA, Lahore
005	SATLUJ COTTON MILLS	WAREHOUSE INCHARGE	1943-47	OKARA, Lahore
006	HINDUSTAN MOTORS LTD	PROJECT MANAGER	1947-49	CALCUTTA
007	DALMIA'S MINAXI CHEMICALS LTD	MANAGER	1949-50	GUNTOOR, AP
008	PB HIGHER SECONDARY SCHOOL	PRINCIPAL	1950-71	SURAJGARH
009	PC INTER COLLEGE, FARAH	DIRECTOR	1971-73	MATHURA, AGRA
010	AGRAWAL COLLEGE, BALLABHGARH	MANAGING TRUSTEE	1973-76	BALLABHGARH, FARIDABAD

Chart-3: AWARDS AND ACHIEVEMENTS

SR.NO.	***AWARDS AND RECOGNITION***	***YEAR***	***PLACE***
001	***FIRST GRADUATE OF SURAJGARH***	***1932***	***SURAJGARH***
002	***FIRST POSTGRADUATE OF SURAJGARH***	***1936***	***SURAJGARH***
003	YOG ACHARYA	1945	OKARA,LAHORE
004	SAHITYA RATNA	1956	ALLAHBAD
005	AYURVEDA RATNA	1961	ALLAHBAD
006	VYAKARAN SAHITYA ACHARYA	1964	BHU, BANERAS
007	BHARTIYA SHIKSHA RATNA	1971	DELHI
008	SAMAJ RATNA	1974	JODHPUR
009	BRAHMAN RATNA	1976	JHUNJHUNU

Chart-4:List of photographs in the book

Famous lines often quoted By Headmasterji.

"Education is my birth right. And distribution of education is every student's."

"I have riches of Education. And believe me it increases with every bit ofgiving to others. Whosoever wishes totake it, can come to me and collect it for free."

"Educate women in family and be sure that your three generation are educated."

"God has been kind enough tome, for he has given me a mission of lifetime- making everyone literate whosoever comes to me for it."

"The real sun will rise and rise high enough for all to affirm, and so will the name of my Surajgarh, the day Surajgarh will be high on education."

"Destiny has already been decided the day you were born, whatyou can do is work and decide the path to reach your destiny. Education is the map of destiny you want to attain in your life. So be educated."

"Donation of education is greatest and noblest donation in this world."

"Life is a beautiful journey and education is the ticket to enjoy this journey.

Else you will have to travel like a passenger without ticket."

“I am sowing the seeds of nurturing education sapling in Surajgarh, and one day the tree of education will stand tall enough to be noticed.”

“I am not a magician though- but education is the magic wand –which can dramitacally change anybody’s life. I am an educationalist, and some people call me magician.”

“Good education is the base of the tall building in form of you, which people will notice in future.”

“Spectaclestongue and books are probably the best friends a teacher can have.”

“Education has all the power and you remain powerful throughout once you are educated.”

“Education is the key to success locked in the darkness of you future.”

“Education is the lantern fuel which will enlighten you all through you life for free.”

Sanskrit sloks often recited by headmasterji:

Na chor haryam, Na cha raj haryamNa bhratu bhajyam Na cha bharkariVyaye krute vardhart ev nityaamVidya dhanam sarva dhane pradhanam

Meaning: No one can steal it, not authority can snatch, Not divided in brothers, not heavy to carry, As you consume or spend, it increases; as youshare, it expands, Education (Vidhya) is the best wealth among all thewealth anyone can have.

2. Vidya dadati vinayam, Vinaya dadati paatrataam, paatratva dhanamaapnoti, dhanaat dharmam tatatsukham.

Meaning: Education gives Humility, Humility gives Character, from character one gets wealth, from wealth one gets righteousness, in righteousness there is joy.

3. Prayatnen kaarye susidhir jananaam, Prayatnen sad-budhi vridhir-jananaam, Prayatnen yudhe jaya: syajananaam, Prayatno vidheya: prayatno vidheya:

Meaning: Hardwork makes people successful, Hardwork strenghtens the wisdom, Hardwork makes us win in the battle, So, keep hardworking, keep doing hardwork...

4. yeshan na vidya, na tapo na daanang nagyanag na sheelang, na guno nadharmang, te mrityoloke bhuvibharbhuta manushyarupen mrigash-

Meaning: charanti jisme na vidya hai, na tap hai na daan karne kipravriti hai, na gyan hai na sheetalta hai, na koi gunhai na hi dharm ki jaankari hai, aise manushyamriyulok me charte huye pashu ke samaan hain

http://jan.ucc.nau.edu/~sj6/pandeychaptertwo.pdf

PART I

INTRODUCTION TO NATIVE & CLAN

Chapter 1

Introduction to Surajgarh

Points covered

- Janmsthan- Surajgarh
- Geographic Location
- Surajgarh: Gateway of Shekhawati
- Surajgarh Fort: Foundation
- Educational Environment of Shekhawati before independence
- History of rulers
- Formation of Surajgarh
- History of 100 yrs before 1900 AD
- Year 1900-2000
- History of education at Surajgarh
- Leader in education at Surajgarh
- Old Sanskrit era
- Ayurvedic Era
- Surajgarh leadership in Sanskrit schools and ayurveda
- Geographic Location- Map
- Historical background

Ref: http://www.shekhawati.in/history-of-shekhawati/

Chapter 1

Introduction to Surajgarh

Culture of a place is a reflection of its society. The culture of Surajgarh is fascinating and captivating. It tells us about the people of the place, their lifestyle and their beliefs. Observing the culture of Surajgarh gives one a fair idea about the traditions and practices that are still followed by the locals. The festivals, the events, the attractions, all reflect the culture of Surajgarh in one way or the other. Tourism has picked up in the last decade or so and the local people are generally quite friendly towards the tourists.

About Shekhawati

Nestled in the dusty and semi desert part of Rajasthan is a group of towns that constitute the enchanting and mesmerizing colourful region of Shekhawati, the much-acclaimed open-air art gallery of Rajasthan. Shekhawati meaning the 'the land of Shekha's clan' derives its name from Rao Shekha (1433 A.D.-1488 A.D.)

Shekhawati is a desert area in Rajasthan and has tremendous historical significance for Indians. It has several references in the epic of Mahabharata and is widely believed that the 'Vedas', the holy text of the Hindus, was written in this part of the country. The Shekhawat Rajputs were the dominant rulers of the area and the magnificent forts and havelis of the region were built by them. In fact, the place is named after Rao Shekha, its erstwhile ruler. Shekhawati is known as the 'open art gallery of Rajasthan' for its multiple forts, havelis and other historical structures. Famous among these are the Haveli Nadine Prince, Morarka Haveli Museum, Dr. Ramnath A Podar Haveli Museum, Jaganath Sanghania Haveli and the Khetri Mahal. The Haveli Nadine Prince dates back to 1802, currently owned by a French artist who has converted it into an art gallery and cultural centre. Dr. Ramnath A Podar Haveli Museum has several galleries on Rajasthani culture, whereas the Morarka Haveli Museum has a 250 year old fort. The Khetri Mahal dates back to 1770, considered to be a very sophisticated structure with a magnificent view.

Among the famous forts of the region are Mandwa Fort, Mukundgarh Fort and Dundlord Fort. The Mandwa Fort is now a heritage hotel. The Dundlord Fort has a world famous library of European paintings. The Mukundgarh Fort is a sprawling palace spread out over an area of close to 8000 sq m replete with ancient courtyards, verandahs and balconies.

Shekhawati also has some unique mosques and a deer sanctuary. It is quite common among tourists to travel locally on a camel safari in order to enjoy the desert. Many of the palaces in the region have been converted into hotels and can offer a unique hospitality experience to visitors. There is a desert festival held every year in the month of February which attracts large crowds to see the various cultural programs held as part of the festival. Known as the Shekhawati Festival, it is held generally in February. Jointly organised by the State Tourism Department and the District Administrations of Sikar, Churu and Jhunjhunu, Nawalgarh is the main venue of the festival.

The festival provides a glimpse into the rural lifestyle of the people of this region. Camel and jeep safaris are also part of the festivities. Rural games, haveli competitions, cultural events, farm visits and fireworks are other attractions of this festival which will be spread over four venues, viz. Nawalgarh, Sikar, Jhunjhunu and Churu. The best time to visit Shekhawati is the winter season from November to February. Temperatures during the summer months can touch 43^{0} Celsius.

In Shekhawati there were only Kharif crops such as bajra, moong and moth. Camels were used for ploughing. Hence, Bajra is the staple food of this region. People relish Bajre ki roti & Gur(Jaggery), Bajre ki Khichdi, Moong Moth ki dal & Wada.

History of Shekhawati:

In the medieval era, Rajasthan stood divided into five large and several smaller principalities. The big 5 were Amber (Jaipur), Bikaner, Jaisalmer, Jodhpur (Marwar) and Udaipur (Mewar). The first two kingdoms shared the region which was destined to become so rich in murals. The founder of beautiful Shekhawati region was MahaRao Shekha Ji, a descendant of the illustrious Kachhawaha Rajput clan who held Amber-Jaipur for centuries. The chieftains of Shekhawati were the descendants of Baloji, the third son of Raja Udaikaranof Amber, who succeeded to the throne of in 1389.

The story of MahaRao Shekha Ji's birth is interesting. Mokul Ji was a 15th century chieftain in the Amber territory who was much troubled because he had no son. In those days, it was almost sinful for a ruler to die without an heir, for who would sit on the throne after his death? So having heard a lot about the miraculous powers of the Muslim saint Sheikh Burhan Chisti, Mokul Ji and his wife decided to pay the man a visit. With the blessings of the Sheikh, a son was born to the Rajput couple. Mokul Ji christened his boy Shekha, who was to become the founder of Shekhawati or the 'Garden of Shekha', an important part of the surface of Rajputana.

MahaRao Shekha Ji(ruled 1433-88) was the chieftain of Amarsar in Amber where he refused to pay tribute to the Kachhawaha rulers of Amber-Jaipur. Thus breaking away, he proclaimed sovereignty in 1471 AD. In the following years Shekhawati comprised of a disparate sequence of small fiefdoms locally known asthikanas, the notable of which were Sikar, Khetri Nawalgarh, Dundlod, Mandawa and Parasrampura. However, the chieftains of Shekhawati retained a nominal loyalty to the Amber (Jaipur) State, who in turn honored them with hereditary titles. It was more like they were in alliance with, rather than subservient to the Amber throne and it was probably due to this exposure to the beautiful courts of Amber-Jaipur that Shekhawati's forts and havelis (mansions) came to be decorated gloriously with murals. Anyway, the Shekhawati-Amber power equation is best expressed in James Tod's words: "The history of the Shekhawat confederation, which springing from the redundant feudalistic Amber, through the influence of age and circumstances, has attained a power and consideration almost equaling that of the parent state; and although it posses neither written laws, a permanent congress, nor any visible or recognized head, subsists by a sense of common interest."

As the Mughal Empire fell into decline after the death of Aurangzeb in 1707, the descendants of MahaRaoShekha Ji, who had already spread themselves in the east of the Aravallis, began to encroach the west and north through the Udaipurwati and Sikar gaps in the hills.

Before the Shekhawat Rajputs could properly establish their fiefdoms on a large scale, the land had to bewrested from the ruling Muslim nawabs (governors). The latter had secured their estates with the help of the Delhi sultans who were in the country until 1526 when Babur came and routed them. Anyway, theShekhawats were there to announce their arrival on the scene. In 1730 Jhunjhunu was seized by SardulSingh (ruled 1730-52). The following year he allied with Sheo Singh (ruled from 1721), the powerful ruler ofSikar and evicted the nawab of Fatehpur, Sardar Khan. Rohella Khan and Sardar Khan were descendants of Kaim Khan and therefore called Kaimkhanis, were the most powerful of the nawabs of the region. With their defeat, important portions of territory thus got added to Shekhawati. By 1732, these two Shekhawatithakurs (chieftains), Sardul Singh Ji and Sheo Singh Ji, had carved a big niche for themselves. They grew very powerful and many of the other thakurs looked up to them for help.

Shekhawati was flourishing, and the signs were obvious. The Shekhawat Rajputs got their forts and palaces covered with murals.

Jhunjhunu lorded over by Sardul Singh, was richest and the most happening thikana of the painted region. It served as the capital of the new and extended Shekhawati. After Sardul Singh's death in 1752, the estatewas divided equally among his five sons – Zorawar Singh, Kishan Singh, Akhey Singh, Nawal Singh and Keshri Singh. Jhunjhunu thus came to be known as the Panchpana – the five estates. But it did not stay so for long, because Akhey Singh died without leaving an heir. His share was to be redistributed among the other four. Sardul Singh had made for himself a big empire, for even at the end of it all, the sons got big chunks and ruled autonomously. Zorawar Singh inherited Taen, Gangiyasar and Malsisar; Kishan Singh got Khetri and Alsisar; Nawal Singh founded Nawalgarh and Mandawa; and Keshri Singh Bissau and Dunlod. The thakurs of every village in the region covered by the Panchpana were all descended from one or other of these men.

In course of time, the cake that Jhunjhunu was got cut further. The most prosperous region remained Mandawa and Nawalgarh, because of the excellent relations they shared between them. On the other extreme was Bissau, which in the hands of Keshri's grandson Thakur Shyam Singh.

From the turn of the 19th century till about 1822, a vast amount of trade was diverted through Shekhawati and more and more merchants got attracted into the region. This was the meeting point of the camel caravans from the Middle East, China and India. Trade in opium, cotton and spices flourished. The merchant community that grew then is still a prominent class in the Indian society today – the marwaris. The huge sums of money that they dished out was to pay for the sheer volume of artistic expression that adorns the walls of Shekhawati. These marwaris and banias (traders by profession, not necessarily belonging to any particular region) built palatial havelis for themselves and memorials for their ancestors. For, the haveli was to a bania what the fort was to a Rajput. These havelis were like fortified houses which walled in the lives of the women, who spent most of their days in the zenana (women's apartments), built around an inner courtyard. The men conducted their business on the white cotton mattresses of their sitting rooms. The marwaris also financed many temples, gardens, baolis (step wells) and dharamshalas (caravansaries) for the people. It was obvious that Shekhawati was growing prosperous, thanks to the industrious trading classes. But greater wealth was yet to flow into Shekhawati.

The flourishing cross-desert commerce wilted away as the British political set up grew stronger. More and more stress was being laid on the ports of Bombay and Calcutta instead, to establish monopolies for the East India Company. By the 1820s and 30s, it became more than clear that the future of trading did not lie in the sands of Rajasthan. But the marwaris of Shekhawati would not be so easily put down. Leaving their native land, the menfolk migrated all the way to the upcoming eastern colonial capital to put their trading genius to good use. Here too, they flourished which inspired more of their brethren to join them in an alien land and by the end of the 19th century, the marwaris had carved a pretty big niche for themselves in the economic sphere in Calcutta. Similarly, they took position in Bombay, Surat and Hyderabad too.

Nothing in the history of India compares with the successful migration of the Shekhawati merchants. According to an American sociologist "it is estimated that more than half the assets in the modern sector of the Indian economy are controlled by the trading castes originating in the northern half of Rajasthan". and of these, a majority originates in just a dozen little towns of Shekhawati.

http://www.shekhawati.in/history-of-shekhawati/

After remaining independent for a long time the Shekhawati confederacy started paying tribute to the state of Jaipur from the beginning of the 18th century. In 1836-37, the Shekhawati Brigade was formed to repulse the attack by the Marathas. However, the brigade was disbanded in 1842. A part of the brigade was transformed into the 13th Rajput Regiment of which Maharaja Madho Singh became honorary colonel in 1904.

James Tod refers to Shekhawati as Shekhawat Federation, thereby implying a union of the thikanas and jagirs of Shekhawati. Tod observes that Shekhawati attained a power and consideration almost equal to that of the present state. It had no written laws, neither a permanent confederation nor any visible head, nor a sense of common interest. There was no system of policy in the Shekhawati confederation. Thus, the jagirs and thikanas of Shekhawati were independent in practice in their territories. Tod and many other indigenous writes have showered praises on the Rajput rulers of Shekhawati and glamourised their rule. However, some recent studies have highlighted the excesses and atrocities committed by the thikanedars, jagirdars and bhomias on the people. The foundation of Shekhawati was characterized by the gradation of thikanas and jagirs. Sikar, Khetri, Patan and Bissau were ranked as thikanas of the first category. In the second category were the thikanas of Nawalgarh, Dundlod, Mukundgarh, Alsisar, Malsisar, Mandawa, etc. The thikanas of Hikha, Dabri, Sultana, Chankari, Tani, Gongiasar, Balria and Ponkh were included in the third category. Thus, the thikanas varied in terms of their status and relations with the state of Jaipur. There were also differences in terms of their size, revenue, and power enjoyed by them.

Clearly, there was a three dimensional administrative setup: (1) the Thikanas, (2) the Jaipur Raj, and (3) the British Raj. There was conflict between the Jaipur Raj and the thikanas as the later claimed their autonomy, and the former claimed its sovereignty over them. The British always took advantage of this conflict by way of arbitration between the two. The thikanedars of Shekhawati asserted that the Khiraj payed to the Jaipur darbar was based on their kin ties rather than sovereignty of the ruler. The Jaipur state, however, considered the jagirdars as ijaradars, hence denied hereditary rights to them over the thikanas. The famous c.w. Wills report also supported this view held by the Jaipur darbar.

The British had reserved for itself the right to arbitrate between the Jaipur state and the thikanas. In the matters of *zakat* and *shariat* the state of Jaipur was never allowed to interfere in the thikanas. The British generally favoured the stand taken by the thikanas. Yet, the British treated them as part of Jaipur. The thikanas were allowed to enjoy a great deal of autonomy. Due to such ambiguity and complexity of the situation the darbar and the thikanas could never form an united front against the Raj. In 1931 the population of Shekhawati was 601,814, and it was 733,142 in 1941. After 1941 one does not find a mention of Shekhawati as a region in official records in 1951 and onwards. According to 1941 census the population of Sikar thikana was 261,356, and of khetri it was 175,260. Sikar consisted of 430 villages with an annual income of Rs.7 lakh and khetri had 258 villages with an annual income of Rs. 5 lakhs.Sikar, as it is evident from our discussion, was the second largest town in the state of Jaipur with a population of 21,523 in 1901, of which 60 per cent were Hindus and 35 per cent were Muslims. The Rao Raja of Sikar managed an anglo-vernacular school, which was attended in 1904 by 90 boys only. The Rao Raja also maintained a hospital with a provision for 16 in-patients. There were also seven indigenous schools in the town. The total population of Sikar chiefship was 1,73,485 in 1901, of which Hindus were 85 percent and Muslims 13 per cent. The income of the chiefship was about Rs. 8 lakh and the tribute paid to the Jaipur darbar was Rs. 41,200.

Casteism, Feudalism and Peasantry in Shekhawati

To understand the power structure of the region, it is necessary to understand the society and polity of the period preceding independence. The system of tenure--jagirs, theoretically speaking, existed in the states of Rajputana. Samir Amin calls such a system – 'tributary feudalism'.

Since the Jagirdars of Shekhawati belonged to the Kacchawa clan of Rajputs, they were also guided by patrimonial ties, but the hierarchy of jagirs undermined patrimonial brotherhood.

Thus, equality and inequality, in other words, kinship and power were inbuilt aspects of the feudal system. Moreover, the tenurial grants turned to be hereditary in practice. There was also nexus between feudalism and caste. Besides differential land, revenue, corresponding with caste hierarchy, there was also differential involvement of castes and groups in the affairs of jagirs and thikanas. The main castes, sub-castes and other social groups comprised of Brahmins, Rajputs, Mahajans, Kayasthas, Sikhs, Muslims, Jains, etc. All these groups were sub-divided into several sub-groups. The upper castes in the state of Jaipur, in general, were ahead of other castes in generating social and political awakening among people. The well-known leaders of this period were Chiranji Lal Mishra, Mal Chandra Sharma, Kapur Chand Patni, Hira Lal Shastri, Chiranji Lal Aggarwal, Hans Deb Roy, Arjun Lal Sethi, Harish Chandra Sharma, etc. In the 1930s and the 1940s these leaders, all coming from upper castes, dominated the affairs of the Praja MandaI. JamunalalBajaj, a well-known national Gandhian leader, belonged to a village in Sikar district, gave a positive direction to the Praja Mandal. These leaders organised the masses against the cruel feudal system in the state of Jaipur.

Clearly, there was a nexus between castes, feudalism, and peasantry in the sense that all castes including peasantry were associated with feudalism, though differently. Feudalism was a social formation, a system of polity and administration and economy. Jats were a principal agricultural caste in Sikar district. Being the principal agricultural caste, they had to bear the maximum brunt of feudalism and were victims of unscientific and arbitrary system of collection of land revenue like *batai, kunta, ijara,* etc. and innumerable taxes and cesses. The functionary and some other castes were forced to render *begaar* in the form oflabour at the jagirdar's personal farms. As aresult of all this the peasant castes, particularly, the

Jats mobilised themselves and demanded social equality withthe upper castes.

Socio-political Awakening in Shekhawati

Due to above situation several peasant and caste organizations emerged in the Shekhawati region. The Jat leadership was conspicuously ahead of others in the peasant organisations and peasant movements. Leaders like Harlal Singh, Ladu Ram Kisari, Choudhary Ghasi Ram, Choudhary Desh Raj, Netram Singh, Hardev Singh Pathsari, Bhairon Singh Togla, Beg Raj Singh Mandori, etc. led the Jat movement. SirChottu Ram, the greatest Jat leader of the period, also visited the Shekhawati region and blessed the peasant leadership. The Jat Sabha and the Jat peasant leadership were coterminous phenomena. The Jat Sabha and the Jat panchayatand the members of these organisations also dominated the Kisan Sabha and the Kisan panchayat. Brahamins, Mahajans and Kayasthas were involved in the administration of the Jaipur state and the jagirs and the thikanas of Sikar chief ship, hence they did not actively participate in the Kisan movement barring some notable cases. The non-Jat leaders, Ram Joshi, Narottam Joshi, namely, Jamuna Lal Bajaj, Laduetc. were against the feudal system in general, but they were not actively involved as leaders of the kisan movement. The leadership coming from other castes was also discouraged by the hegemonic dominance of the Jats in the Kisan movement. The Jats of Shekhawati, and in particular their religious saints, undertook tours of the region and organized fairs and festivals in the 1920s. All-India Jat MahaSabha became active in the region. The first conference of Kisans in the region was organised at Khandela in 1925. In 1930, Shekhawati Jat Maha Sabha was formed on the pattern of the All-India Jat Maha Sabha. Later on, the Jat ShikshaSamiti was formed to educate the Jat youth. A Jat Vidhayarthi Parishad was also started during this period. In several thikanas and jagirs of Shekhawati Jat Panchayats and JatSabhas were formed. In 1932, a big conference of the All India Jat MahaSabha was held at Jhunjhunu. In January 1935, a Jat PrajapatiMahayagya was organised at Sikar. In 1938, at thePushkar *mela* (fair) an organisation by the name of JatKrishak Sudharak was formed. All these events were organized as social mobilizations of the Jats in the region.

These efforts gave a definite shape and character to the Jat- peasant leadership to start a compaign of no taxes and no*lag-bags* and *begaar* to the thikanedars.

Hence, four social components of Shekhawati were: (1) Rajputs (Jagirdarsand Bhomias) *i* (2) Jats (peasants); (3) upper castes other than Rajputs (literati and economic dominants); and (4) lower castes (artisans and functionaries).

Climate& Culture of Shekhawati

Shekhawati has a dry climate with hot summers, cold winters and a short monsoon. Winter starts by about the middle of November and continues till about the beginning of March. Summer follows thereafter and extends upto the end of June. The South-West monsoon season is from

July to mid Sept. The period from mid-Sept. to mid-Nov. constitutes the post monsoon season.

June is the hottest month of the year. The mean daily maximum temperature in this month is 41.1 C and the mean daily minimum temperature is 28.2 C. In May and June the heat is intense and on some days the maximum temperature rises upto about 46 C.

After mid-November both day and night temperatures decreases rapidly till January, which is the coldest month.

The average annual rainfall in the Shekhawati is 455.5 mm. The rainfall increases from the North-West towards the South-East. During the South-West monsoon period the rainfall constitutes about 75% of the annual rainfall, July being the rainiest month. The variation in the rainfall from year to year is large; on an average there are 27 rainy days.

Fairs and festivals in Shekhawati

Teej – Shukla Paksh tritya (July/August) to Bhadra Pad Shukla Ekadashi (Jal Jhulni Ekadashi)

This festival marks the advent of monsoon. In the month of Shravana, swing is hung from tree tops and the women are seen joyfully dressed and enjoying the cool breeze after a long hot summer. They sing songs of love and welcome the rains and even their swings are decorated with flowers.

Gangaur- Chaitra Tritya (March/April)

A festival dedicated to Gauri, a manifestation of the goddess Parvati, where maidens and married woman join in procession carrying beautifully adorned wooden images of the goddess, through the streets and praying for the well being of their husbands or asking for a husband of their dreams.

Hindola

From Shravani Poornima – Raksha Bandhan to Janmashtami, there is a tradition to have hindolas in all temples

Chatda Chauth

Also known as Ganesh Chaturthi is celebrated on Bhadra pad shukla chaturthi. It is considered as "Sinjhara" for the men folk. They wear new clothes and play Gindad

Holi

Holi is celebrated from Basant Panchmi to Dhuleti. Every night they play Dhap which is a round, big instrument with a diameter of 5 to 10 feet. They sing Dhamaal and Gindad. Males are dressed in female outfits as Bhaand and play Gindad. There are Gindad competitions also. On the day of Holi, they prepare a symbol of Holika & Prahlad, for which they gather stems & logs of trees and then pyre is created and Bigger logs of holika & Prahalad.

Besides that the regular festivals like Diwali, Dusshera and Makar Sakranti are celebrated.

The Shekhawati folk songs reminds of the glorious past of shekhawati.

Map of Shekhawati

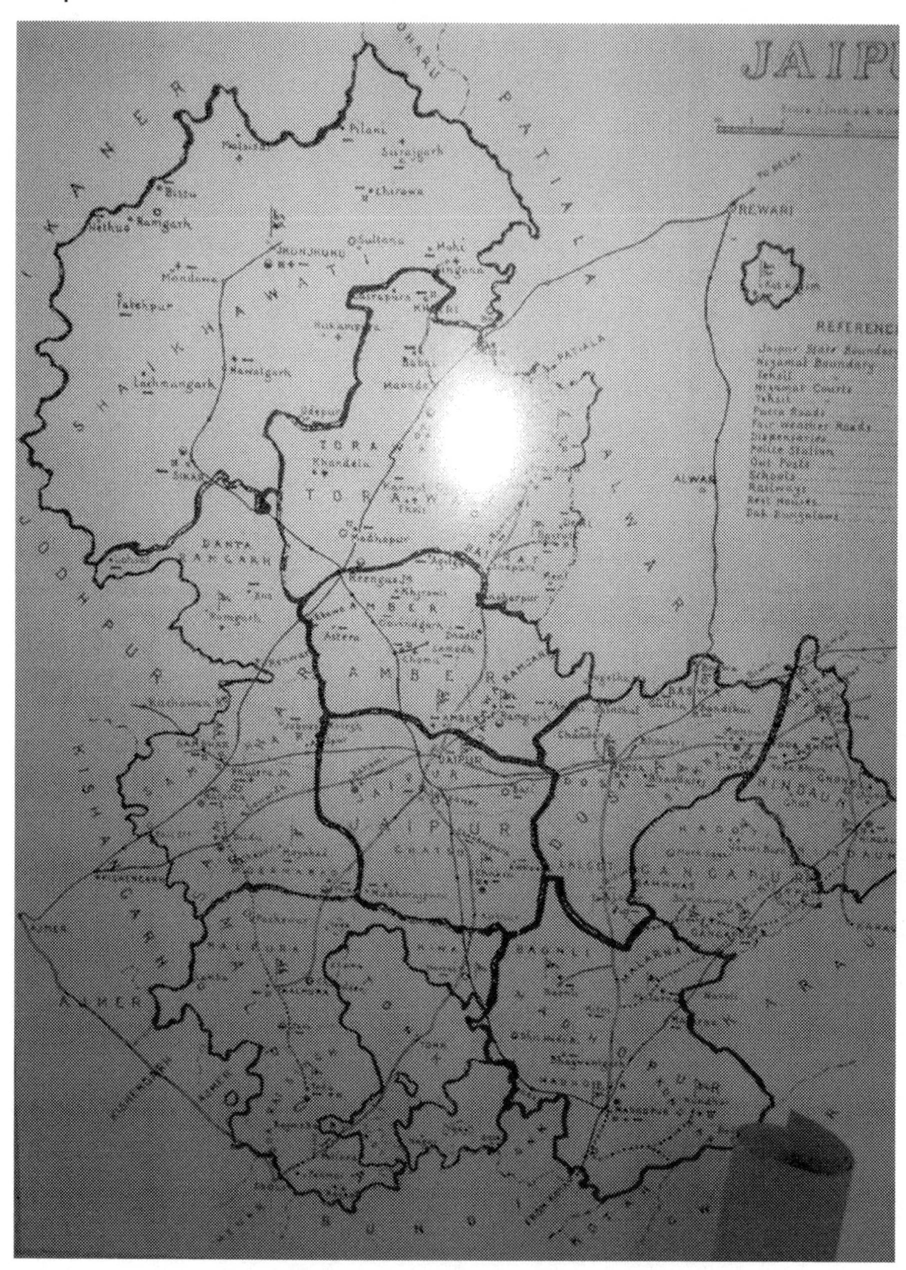

Picture Reference 1: Map of Shekhawati region

Map of Surajgarh

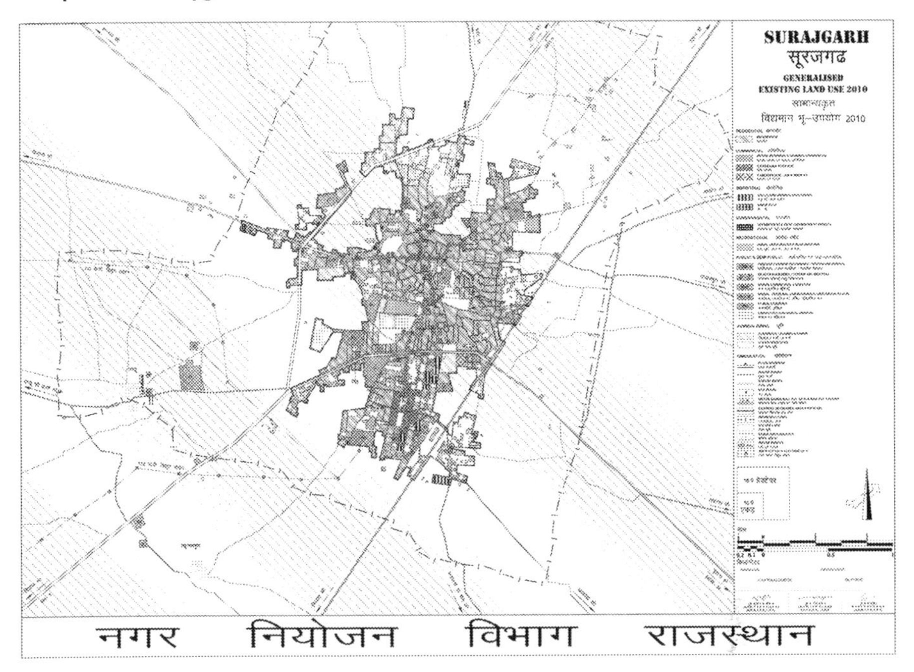

Picture Reference 2: Map of Surajgarh

Geographic Location and History of Surajgarh

Surajgarh is a Town in Surajgarh Mandal, Jhunjhunu District, Rajasthan State., India. Surajgarh is located at 28.32°N 75.73°E. It has an average elevation of 280 metres (918 feet). As of 2001 India census, Surajgarh had a population of 18,857. Surajgarh is 37.5 km far from its District Main City Jhunjhunu. It is 200 km far from its State Main City Jaipur and 180 Km away from Delhi, capital of India. The town is famous for its Fort and architectural Marvel. The old name of Surajgarh used to be 'ADICHA ki Dhani', which was founded by Adichwala Brahmins, who migrated from Kalanoor in Haryana and then gradually with the development, the place was then called "ADICHA".Established in 1780 by ThakurSuraj Mal, Bissau (Thikana) Shekhawat (Sadhani clan) the township of Surajgarh came up with the construction of the fort, for the construction of the fort not only offered employment to the people from the neighboring villages, but after its completion also offered a safe sanctuary from marauding bandits and invading armies. Surajgarh got established in 1780.

Surajgarh: Gateway of Shekhawati

Surajgarh is situated in the north-east of Rajasthan and shares the border with Haryana and Punjab. Hence, it is called "**Gateway of Shekhawati from North India**". The visitors to Shekhawati always take the route through Surajgarh only. The opium which was produced in Malwa region of India was imported to China, through the same route. During ancient times, this used to be the busiest route throughout the year. In those days Bhiwani used to be the main Wholesale Market (Mandi) for the farmers of Punjab, and hence, thousands of camels loaded with grains would pass through this route to reach Bhiwani.

Surajgarh Fort: Foundation

Surajgarh was founded on 1st August 1777 (Bhadwa Sudhi Dashami, Vikram Samvat 1834) by King of Bissau, Surajmal. King Surajmal along with his ministers visited this region, where they witnessed an eye opening incident. They saw a cow fighting with the beast whole through the night to save its newly born calf, which impressed king Surajmal. He got convinced that the place where the animal like cow could fight the odds, must be the "Land of the Bravehearts" and hence he decided to build the fort there and named it after himself as "Surajgarh". Later this was expanded by the son of Surajmal, Shyam Singh, who also constructed the 20 feet high wall around the whole village. In 1939 when Jaipur state railway was extended from Jhunjhunu to Luharu, Surajgarh also got connected through railways.

During the reign of Bishan Singh ji, the Post and Telegraph office was set up in Surajgarh and the post was sent to Pilani weekly from this post office. Surajgarh was important trade centre, just next to Bhiwani. The copper coins were also minted here. In 1850, "Jeevan Mandi" was founded by Thakore Jeevan Singhji, in consultation with Lok Ram ji Ghagshyan, who was the grandfather of Ram Bilasji.

Currently there are 25 temples, 20 guesthouses and 2 chatris. There are lot of Sivalayas and Hanuman temple. Now, the Surajgarh fort has been converted to a five star hotel.

Educational Environment of Shekhawati before independence

Jaipur state of those times was the centre of education and had best educational facilities. But this was restricted to Jaipur state only and there was no effort to develop other parts of Shekhawati, in the field of education. The rulers of Jaipur, had a doubt that, in case of the development of the other areas of Shekhawati, the importance of the Maharaja college of Jaipur would be reduced. Hence, in the other towns of Shekhawati region like Surajgarh and Chirawa, there were no formal schools, rather they were more like Gurukuls which were called "Chatshalas" and Sanskrit and Hindi schools were under the administration of Marwari Seths. There were only Primary, Middle and High schools in the Shekhawati region and the two exams-Upper Primary examination and Jaipur Middle school examination were conducted for these schools by "Sarvajanik Shiksha Vibhag" of Jaipur, to have control over these schools. The Jaipur state had no support to these schools except that they would send the Inspector of schools for inspection purpose, as they conducted the above mentioned two exams. Education and Public welfare was considered as the responsibility of the Thakurs or the landlords of those tehsils under Jaipur state. Moreover, except for the few broad minded rulers, none of the rulers of Shekhawati, would encourage education in their areas, as they considered educated and awakened public as the hurdle to their despotic rule. Their relation with Public would be confined to only recovering lagan, taxes and forcing them for labor. Due to the efforts of some regional business houses, the education had got impetus in Shekhawati. Decade after the year 1916 witnessed the importance of English and Hindi education in shekhawati. During those days only, the high schools of Khetri and Sikar, Middle schools in Ramgarh, Fatehpur and Chirawa were established. Besides that, in Surajgarh, Mandrela, Nawalgarh, Pilani, Jhunjhunu, Bissau etc. the upper Primary Schools were established. The people behind these developments were- Birlas, Ruias, Poddars, Somanis, Rungtas and Jhunjhunuwalas, who were all into business. GD Birla and Jamna lal Bajaj, made a policy to spread education and called it "Rajputana Shiksha Mandal." During that time RaiBahadur Surya mal Shiv Prasad of Chirawa, started 110 Chatshalas, Mahajani and Hindi education in the near-by villages in Chirawa.

Surajgarh and Mahabharat Connection

Pandavas in as per great Indian epic "Mahabharat" after the defeat inthe Dhrutkrida (gambling game played by kings) spent 12 yr in forest and one year after that in Agyatvas(hideouts). They spent one year in kingdom of king Virat. The kingdom of Virat extended from Jhunjhunu district to Kot Kasim(109 kms in north,) Jhunjhunu to ajmer 184 kms in west, Ajmer to Banas and upto Chambal river 229 kms in south. The capital was Bairat.

Surajgarhand RiverSaraswati

Saraswati river used to flow from place in between Surajgarh and Khetri.

Surajgarh and Chavanprash:

Chavanprash is today best medicine from ayurveda. The inventor of Chavanprash was rishi.

Dhora hills - the revered hill ranges, bordering Surajgarh and Haryana border, is famous for rishi chavan ashram, this was the place where chavanprash was formulated for the first time in the Indian ayurveda, and it was at Surajgarh. This is mentioned in the Mahabharat in Vanprast episode.

Khetri is today famous in whole world for the Copper mines and government of india Hindustan Zinc ltd- copper project-khetri., the presence of the copper hills and mines indicates that once in the history, there was a volcanic eruption that led to formation of the copper and other mineral rich hill in this region.

The Saraswati river water was best for medicinal purpose and hence the water of Surajgarh till today is a natural healer and rich in minerals, naturally purified by copper and other minerals. The soil here is very fertile. And a lot of herbal plants andtrees were natural habitant of Surajgarh area. It is evident from the chavanprash. and there has been a history of Ayuveda and vaidhyaji (ayurvedic doctors.) people use to come from distant places to take treatments to Surajgarh.

Khetri- Surajgarh areal distance is merely 30-35kms.

Because of the presence of rishi munis in this region, this place is very peaceful, since many saints have done penance here. Therefore the people here are religious minded, because of the effect of such environment, there is purity of air, water and soil in this region. The mind and soul of people in this region are very pure because of mantra chanting done by the saints here thousands of years ago.

The air and ambience in and around Surajgarh has inner and deep peace because of the yagna performed by Saints and rishi muni thousands of years ago. The atmosphere of this place is pure, religious and satisfying. The rishi-muni grew lot of herbal medicine/ Jadi-butis in this place. This made the air of the place medically pure. Today though the rishi-munis are no more, but the fragrance in the air is the remedy for many diseases. You will find people mentioning that, "Hawa-Pani" of this region is very salubrious. During rainy season, flow of water is from the top of hills, which carries the properties of minerals like calcium and copper. The same water passes through the crater of the volcano, which existed hundreds of year ago in the Khetri region. It carries the property of copper from the copper mines and also takes the property of the jadi-butis grown in the region, which makes the water medicinal and this increases the life span of people living there.

Culture of Surajgarh

The people of Surajgarh are very religious. Before going out for a journey, they would look for good omen and would pay the tribute to God and Pitra. Well-construction was considered community work and also a way to earn Punya. If the water of the well that was dug, would be sweet, then they would hold rati-jaga, to pay the gratitude to Lord Hanuman. Besides the religious value, these well were like the women club, as they would gather there and discuss all sorts of things & especially gossips. So, wells became centre of community life.

Chapter 2

Gaur Brahmins and Ghagshyans

Points covered

- Gaur Brahmins
- Shashans
- Ghagshyan Clan

Chapter 2

Gaur Brahmins and Ghagshyans

Ghagshyan - The Prominent Gaur Brahmin Family

Who are Gaur Brahmins?

Gaur Brahims are the Brahmins originated from a small village of West Bengal and Bangladesh border. The name of that village is GAUR or GOUR located at 24°52′N, 88°08′E near the Indo-Bangladesh international border. It was founded by Lakshmana and was given name as Lakshmanavati, later it was known as Gouda and then Gour. There are different stories about the migration of Gaur Brahmins form West Bengal to Northern India. One of the beliefs is that, after the Muslims invaded Bengal in 11th century the Brahmins moved to the Northern India.

It is believed that Gaur Brahmins were given land and houses by North Indian kings to settle down.

The other belief is that King Parikshit (son of Abhimanu and Uttara) and Grandson of Arjuna, did a Maha Yajna for which he was advised by rishis that to perform that yajna Gaur Brahmans were needed. Thus Parikshit invited Gaur Brahmans from West Bengal. After the Yajna was over, the Brahmins were asked to return to their native place. But King Parikshit requested them to stay back. The Brahmins were worried and told Parikshit that there were no suitable brahmin girls available in his kingdom and hence how would their clan/Vansh continue. On this Parikshit offered them to marry the royal girls(daughters, sisters of royals).

Adi Gour Brahman Gotra & Sashan

1. ***PARVRIDH VASISHT GOTRA***: Tgunayat, Jhimiriya, Jharmriya, Vijaycharan, Gothwal, Haldolia, Nuliwal, Choubepradhan, Diwedi Pradhan, Narwalia, Brahmpuria, Jharmpuria, Mandoria, Kuruskehtri, Sirohiwal, Sarpdama, Kundolia Bhadrawasia, Basotia, Chandolia, Mainwal, Ramhadia, Yanesaria, Gangawasi, Badiwal, Pidra, Safidmiwala.
2. ***VASISHT GOTRA***: Sinwal, Buntolia, Surolia, Kankrit, Natholia, Chulhat, Khairwal, Balachia, Bankolia, Kalaneria, Dhamani Mishra, Baberwal, Narela, Upadhyay, Ghamunia, Gaudwal, Kharwalia, Narnolia, Bidwaria, ChukaniaGoaswami, Sunpatia, Dwijanaia, Gour Grabhiya, Shipuria, Ugratapa, Mishra, Gomani, Atolia, Bijnet, Nachania, Godhria, Pahaktari, Soria, Pharmania, Chrolia, Vayohaal, Naliyariya, Babroliya, Vadgamiya, Varithwal, Silaniya, Diwachiya, Vishmbhra Pradhan, Biyala, Basotia, Kathaliya, Dewliya, Oudhaka, Suthya, Bartar, Gatalima, Simawat, Luniwal Mata, Kulta Japria, Tundwal, Khariwal, Kheriwal, Shorthia, Gill, Gilan, Ramaniya, Changan, Babarwal, Tilawat, Parbati, Gangawat, Adhichwal Joshi.
3. ***GOUTAM GOTRA***: Indoria, Patodia, Dorliya, Duledia, Dohliya, Bayoliya, Nauotania, Ritambhara, Boghar, Gandharwal, Pandyana, Pantiye, Jhuria, Kanoria, Muhanwan, Sathia, Bajre Simmanwal, Pandey, VadibalChoudhary, Jhandoliya Pradhan.
4. ***KASHYAP GOTRA***: Kurusketriya, Gurpuriya, Chulkaniya, Manchaki.
5. ***ATRI GOTRA***: Dhand, Dhigthaliya, Jhadoliya, Jhadoliya Joshi, Tripathi, Ratiwal, Rohitiya, Sirsonia, Vyas, Kankhaliya, Baleriya, Gourpuria, Ghortapa, Sarpddama, Karpundiya, Tusamariya, Didwania, Pandyan, Tandpade, Saagwal, Ganwariya, Jindiya, Kedeliya, Bupadwal, Disawad, Kundhra (Panda), Bariwal, Phulriye, Bariwal Mota Nagwan, Mangloriya, Kasampariya, Dhuncholiya, Maroliya, Nedhaliya, Sankholiya, Sirsaniya, Moteka Tusania, Bheda, Khaksaya, Kriksa, Magas, Mogra, Mandolia, Rame, Rawalma, Sirsania, Mite.
6. ***KRISHNAYA GOTRA***: Nirmal, Rewaliya, Banbarewal, Brahmwedia, Chinkatia, Kakar.
7. ***AGUSTYA GOTRA***: Maharshi, Wajhra, Tapodhara, Utchala, Shuilkpuria, Vidhyadhara, Mayadiya, Salothia, Pihuwal, Vyas.

8. ***KOUSHIK GOTRA***: Dixhit, Bhridwal Pilodha, Lata, Dokwal, Jhimariya, Panwalia, Karirhat, Nagarwal, Phatwariyavyas, Vidhat, Singhwal, Bishkaria, Dana, Chaturvedi, Brijwal, Kanrwal, Bhudoj, Gandhara, Bagarhata, Bahandia, Baghdolia, Ghaghsani, Kotiya, Sayania, Gorkhpuria, Bruhadania, Sirohiwal, Gogani, Mangaloria, Mandalwal, Mathwal, Maharwal Nakare, Pindane, Varsia Chumheth, Untlodia, Kankar, Tigadia, Barad, KamiyaPhutwa, Kalanoria, Kuranwal, Kankar, Vijaycharan Banhaya, Jaisatwara, Bhura, Aastyan, Sankholia.
9. ***BHARDWAJ GOTRA***: Chaklan, Garwal, Dhand, Panchlangia, Indoria, Sindolia, Bhathra, Kaloondia, Gogyan, Sahal, Ghagshyan, Nagwan, Nreda, Tungaria, Wamadolia Dhancholia, Luniwal, Biyala, Marahsiya, Pathak, Gangawat, Kalawatia, Vinwal, Pitrot, Khantwal, Dodwadia, Kharith, Satoria, Dolya, Maloo, Baber, Gilyan, Bijechan, Tikdyant, Paslotia, Chatesaria, Ratelwal, Ramparia, Surolia, Dubey, Nayayasthani, Panwalia, Vadiwal, Kedewal, Choubelal, Godharia, Bijret, Tandolia, Bhiwal, Bawelia, Balochia, Alwaria, Simbhala, Anguthia, Bharthalia, Bhartiya, Chandolia, Mandhania, Chourashi Bayoria, Vijayavani, Nirthalia, Silothia, Kandodhia, Sanwlodia, Vishambhara, Sanklash, Sanpalwal, Madothia, Shivahaya, Dulinhat, Sagwal, Barnaya, Ghijwal, Dabodhia, Pithwal, Sirsoulia, Gosrat, Nigambothia, Tapodhana, Sarpdama, Dantolia, Netwalia, Alselia, Bhadchakki, Tantpradhan, Petwadia, Santoria, Jaywal, Dungarpuria, Natwal, Pihulwal, Galiyan, Gilad, Katwadia, BohariaBhunwal, Galyan, Bankolia, Nudiwal Naharia, Goudia, Mahta, Umrawatia, Gurgamia, Mamdolia, Sandolia, Narhedwal, Niralia, Raiwal Bidahat, Thikaria, Padhia, Choubepradhan, Sindolia, Paladia, Naad, Pawta, Damanil, Kuthia, Sorthya, Kaath, Bardwalia, Bagla, Bima, Bacha, Rahthala, Tharal, Lamba, Dadwadya, Roliwal, Dorwal, Kharwal, Batole, Godhalia, Kamdiwal, Sindolia, Kankrit, Toshyan, Marolia, Bhinda, Jhadodia.
10. ***JAMDAGNI GOTRA***: Ratelwal, Basundwal, Mudahhat.
11. ***VATS GOTRA***: Jhimiria, Balmia, Manjithwal, Bahdolia, Gohria, Nagarwal, Marhata, Sikara, Nagwan, Chouhanwal, Mandawaria, Ghatsaria, Bora, Jhaman.
12. ***MUDGAL GOTRA***: Bawlia, Kasaria, Kakyani, Churolia, Bhinda Joshi, Chulkania, Kakyan, Ramudama.

13. ***PARASHAR GOTRA***: Bagdolia, Khedwal, Hinsaria, Gujarka, Ramgadhia, Jhadsaiya, Narhada, Karnalia, Bhunddat, Lokanda.
14. ***SANDILYA GOTRA***: Haritwal, Chulhiwal, Basundwal, Varundwal, Noongarwal, Pancholia, Bhapyawalia, Parwati, Kalinoora, Rurlwal, Kandwal Pathak, Chaitpuria, Monas, Bhattawalia Tiwari, Sojtama.
15. ***HAARIT GOTRA***: Choumal, Salwal, Sabharia, Kaduvadia, Chohmewal, Khoj, Kandira.
16. ***ANGIRA GOTRA***: Banderwal, Chobedixhit, Gangapuria, Mirchiyan, Chajawat, Jilaraya, Gilad, Nagarwal.
17. ***JAIMINI GOTRA***: Mahtapa, Jamniya, Dharmpuria.
18. ***SHOUNAK GOTRA***: Bhadupota
19. ***OSHESHWAR GOTRA***: Phatwadia.
20. ***SUPRNA GOTRA***: Naguwal, Nigarwal, Nagoora.
21. ***BHIRUGU GOTRA***: Dadwaliye, Rame Pradhan, Abhisay Pradhan, Kalsota, Mandorama.
22. ***HARITAS GOTRA***: Chamhal.
23. ***PIPLAWAN GOTRA:*** Aabyethaya Pradhan, Bhograan Pradhan, Chandolia Pradhan, Bishambara Pradhan.
24. ***VYOG GOTRA***: Kalyan.
25. ***SANKRITYA GOTRA***: Triwedi (Tiwari) Tiwari-Chuliwal-Tiwari, Tayga-Tiwari, Ghurchadhia-Tiwari, Bhadya-Tiwari, Parasaria-Tiwari, Phalodiye-Tiwari, Bhatawala-Tiwari, Rodi-Tiwari, Korak-Tiwari, Bahrodia-Tiwari.
26. ***CHANDRAYAN GOTRA***: Chandnia.
27. ***GALAV GOTRA***: Kath.
28. ***KOTSH GOTRA***: Kakar.

MIGRATION OF GHAGSHYANS

Ghagshyan's has its roots in a place called "Dharadu" in Bhavaniipur (Now Bhiwani) in Punjab province of Pre- independence era (Now Haryana, Kurukshetra in Medieval India), where they were the prominent Gaur Brahmin family. Then Ghagshyan's migrated to different parts of India. One family migrated to Adilabad and is in oil business, since last 5 generations.

Another family of Ghagshyans migrated to Islampur in Jhunjhunu district. I happened to know Shri Chiranjilal ji Sharma, now 83, joined NCC at Pilani and younger Brother joined Navy and is at a senior Post there.

Another Ghagshyan family settled in Agra, Basudevji and Ramkumarji now for three generation. Another family of Vishwanath and Sugan Ghagshyan settled in Delhi. Rajkumar further went to Calcutta.

Srinivasji Ghagshyan's one of the grandson, Shri Anjani Kumarji is still at Surajgarhand the other grandson, Vijay Hariram ji Gahgshyan is settled in Bikaner.

Three sons of Ram Bilasji are settled in Jaipur, the youngest son is settled in Churu.

The author (Sandeep Savitaprakash ji Ghagshyan) is Grandson of Rambilas Gajanand ji Ghagshyan settled in Ahmedabad.

Around 150 years ago, some of the prominent Ghagshyan family's shifted to Jaipur; there were twelve brothers in family, very influential. The place in old Jaipur city Near Govind dev ji ka Chauraha, Chandpole is known as Ghagshyan Barah Bhaiyon ka chauraha.

Barah bahiyon ka Chauraha is a cross road in a walled city, which is situated between Choti Chaupar and Gangauri Bazar. The eleven Ghagshyan brothers and a Muslim, stayed together as a family during the Mughal times. There is a Hanuman temple at this cross road, where all twelve brothers use to meet every evening.

Ghagshyan's and Bissau (Year 1750-1820)

The Shekhawati and its history indicates the prominence of Gahgshyan Gaur Brahmin and their role in Shekhawati right from its formation from Shardul Singh Shekhawat era and formation of the Panch Pana (5 independent Kingdom) Thikana in Shekhawati (Jhunjhunu district).

Raghunathji Ghagshyan was the first Ghagshyan brought in Pachpana thikana in Jhunjhunu Riyasat in 1755 AD. Raghnath ji Ghagshyan's life span extended from 1740-1820. The man responsible for bringing him was Thakur Kesari Singh ji of Bissau Riyasat.

Thakur Kesari Singh was youngest son of Shardul Singh Shekhawat, founded Shekhawati Riyasat. His rule spanned from 1746-1768.

Thakur Suraj mal Singh was born to Kesari Singh in 1755. He later became King of Bissau (Adicha used to come under him). It was in his name the place came to be known as Surajgarh.

PART II

RAMBILAS JI
& HIS FAMILY ROOTS

Chapter 3

Ram Bilas Ji's family roots & Grandfather Lokramji Ghagshyan

Points covered

- Ghagshyan family chart indicating 15 generations
- Grandfather: Pt. Lokramji Ghagshyan
- Gaura Devi & Siddh Mahatma
- Development of Surajgarh
- Thakur Jeevan Singh ji & Lokramji
- Wedding of Lokramji's son Gajanada ji
- Lokramji saviour of cows
- Lokramji & ruler of Mnadawa
- Chappaniya Kaal
- Lokramji's virtues and his distinct qualities

Chapter 3

Ram Bilas Ji's family roots & Grandfather Lokramji Ghagshyan

GHAGSHYAN FAMILY CHART AND 15 GENERATIONS IN SURAJGARH

Picture Reference 3:
Ghagshyan family chart indicating 15 generations

Lok Ram Ji Ghagshyan

Picture Reference 4:
Surajgarh's Rajpurohit, Raj jyotish, Panch Ratna

The grandfather of Lokramji, Shri Hargovindji was the great and learned Brahmin, astrologer and Devi Bhakt and had astature of Minister in the court of Surajmal. He had a son, Gauri Duttji. He portended and declared that the son of Gauri Duttji, would be very famous and would be known all over Shekhawati and Haryana. King to Pauper, all would believe in him. He would be Kulshiromani and would be rich and wealthy and would enjoy all luxuries in his life time. He would be an ideal person like Lord Rama. This son of Gauri duttji was christened "Lok Ram ji". This turned out to be true also.

Lokramji got married to GauraDevi of Saga Village (Narnaul, Haryana), who belonged to Maamroliya family. He had four daughters and two sons- Janki Devi, Hori Devi, Ganga Devi, Nani Devi, Madhav Ramji and Gajanand ji. Madhav Ram ji got married at Tiba Bassai and had no children.

Gaura Devi and siddh mahatma

Lokram ji's son Madhavram ji died at early age. Lokram ji had four daughters after Madhavramji. He was perturbed that he had no son. One day, a mahatma visited Lokramji's house. Only Gaura Devi was at home. Gaura Devi asked mahatma, what he would like to eat. On that Mahatma, asked for water, as he was thirsty. He drank whole water of the filled earthen pot. In those times the means of refrigeration of water were limited and Rajasthan was a hot place, people used to bury the pots in the wet sand, to keep the water cool in the pot. So, was done by Gaura Devi and Mahatma was satiated to drink the cool water. After this mahatma took rest for some time and when got up, asked Gaura Devi, what she wanted. She said, "I have everything but my only son died at early age and now, I have only four daughters. My husband is disturbed and we feel that we would never have a son now." On that Mahatma, who could make predictions, told Gaura Devi that they would have a son, but he would survive only if he withstood three threats to his life. He would be a very lucky child. Mahatma gave her water in Lota to drink water in that and told her that, now the child conceived today, would be a lucky son. This came true and the ninth month from then they had a son, whom they named "Gajanand."

The three threats that the mahatma mentioned was also witnessed by Gaura Devi. After the birth of Gajanada ji, once Gaura Devi took him to the farm, where snake bit him. Fortunately, man working in the nearby farm knew to extract out poison and Gajananda ji was saved.

Second time, as a kid, a pot full of Ghee, spilled over Gajanada ji, which could have suffocated a small kid but his mother noticed that and cleaned him immediately. He was saved second time.

Third time when Gaura Devi had been to Kumbh mela, Gajanadji contracted high fever and his mother was worried. She was sad, one because her son was not well and second because, despite coming to mela, she could not take a dip in the holy water. Suddenly, a sadhu came there and she narrated her problem to him. Sadhu told him to dip the body of Gajanada ji in the holy water, first from the head side and subsequently from the feet side, he would be fine. Surprisingly, sadhu was right and Gajanada ji survived the third threat to his life.

Development of Surajgarh- Lokramji's Advice

Picture Reference 5: Jeevan Mandi, Surajgarh

People would go to Bhiwani Mandi (Haryana) for the trade and because of which taxes would be credited to Haryana and there would be no revenue for Surajgarh and hence no source for development. Thakur Jeevan Singh ji wanted to develop Surajgarh. He took advice from different ministers but was not convinced. Thakur Jeevan Singh ji revered Lok Ramji, so he consulted Lokramji. He advised that since Surajgarh is an agricultural land, we need to focus on that. But then this did not seem to be plausible, as the farming was dependent on good rainfall. So, Thakur ji proposed to implement "Lagan" as a tax. When this proposal was made, all the ministers kept quiet, but Lokramji intervened. He argued," How would farmers pay Lagaan, if the crop yield is not good?" So, he proposed that we must try to find out solution to the scanty rainfall and must arrange for water supply for irrigation. The meeting was adjourned on this note and Lokramji assured that he would get back with the solution and went back home. Lokramji had good relations with Baba Sadinathji, who was a Siddha Mahatma and had meditated in the forest of Surajgarh for years. Thakur ji & Lokramji went to Baba Sadinathji, to seek the solution of the irrigation problem. Baba Sadi nath ji responded, "Lok ramji would give you the solution tomorrow".

After which, Baba called Lokramji and gave him blessings and pointed out the place where they must construct "Bavdi"- a small lake, which would solve the problem of water in the area and would result in good yield. Then, Lokramji met Thakur ji and discussed the same with him. But then they had another issue. When the crop yield was good, the farmers had to travel to Bhiwani Mandi to sell the crop. Hence, Lokramji advised Thakur ji to develop mandi at Surajgarh which would increase the Lagaan. Lokram ji gave it a thought and according to Vastu, advised the place for Mandi development. This Mandi became famous at "Jeevan Mandi".

Jeevan Madi became so famous that the trading started with Haryana, Punjab, Himachal Pradesh and Burma, Tibet and China. As a result of which, the traders of Surajgarh started making money. Surajgarh started developing. 52 traders of Rajgarh, made Surajgarh Mandi as the place of trading(Gaddi). This made Jeevan mandi bigger than Bhiwani Mandi and hence the revenue to Thakur ji increased tremendously.

Then bavdi was constructed with the help of those traders. Specially Chokhiram Kayan gave huge donations for the same.

Lok ram ji used to get the ploughing of the crops / farms bycontracting the labours from jat community. He was very help ful to people from every community like farmers, carpenters, and even shoe makers. He used to give them loan, while paying back the farmers used to offer principle and interest amounts, but he would only take the principle and give back the interest amount back, because of this, people would gift lokramji the urns and potteries of metal prevalent in those days. Lokramji had huge stock of utensils sufficient for serving food to a whole barat(group of 200-300 people) during marriage of the family members and, no catering agency need for the serving utensils.

The King of Surajgarh, Thakur Jeevan Singh and Lokramji

Lokramji was a learned pundit and Sadhak Brahmin. He was devi bhakt and used to do prayer all four sandhyas pujan. Thakur Harisingh (later became king of mandawa) and Jeevan Singh ji (king of Surajgarh) gifted him many land pieces. He had a farm of 100 bigha in the vicinity of Farhat and a big Nohra. He had silver coins and animal wealth. Thakursahab has gifted him five camels and 15 cows. He used to spend his time in puja and was an idealist. He had eternal enlightenment, but he would never misuse it.

In those days the kings would not visit to anybody in his kingdom, rather they would call him to his palace as and when required, but the king of Surajgarh, ThakurJeevansingh would pay a visit to Lokramji's residence personally every night to seek his blessing. Lokramji would pray and meditate at Night and after which he would not touch anybody. So, Thakur ji would do prostrate pranam to Lokramji.

Lokramji's prediction and suggestion to Jeevan Singh ji for the future hier

One day, when Thakur ji came to Lokramji, and as routine he laid down to seek his blessings, Lokramji could intuit that Thakur ji was perturbed as he had no child. So he advised him to adopt Raghubeer Singh ji, son of Thakur Bishan Singh ji(king of **Bissau**). On Lok ramji's advice, Thakur ji adopted Raghubeer Singh ji, who later ruled both Surajgarh and Bissau.

Lokramji's lifespan had been happy and contented. People envy him. They would always try to probe and poke their nose in his matters, in curiosity to know what he was doing and how he was doing that.

Wedding of Lokramji's son (Gajananda ji's) and death of Queen Victoria death on 2nd February 1901

Picture Reference 6: Queen Victoria and the Proclamation of "Day of Mourning" on her death

Lok ram ji was very wise and intelligent. In 1901 AD, when Queen Victoria died, the British ruled India and Surajgarh was under Jaipur Riyasat. So, British declared five days of National Mourning and hence it was ordered that during those five days, no celebrations should be done and there has to be no singing and dancing. The rulers of Shekhawati, including Surajgarh, were forced to follow the orders. Lok ramji's son Gajananda ji's wedding was scheduled during those five days only. As per the Marwadi rituals, they had to sing. This was audible to others and hence enviously, somebody complaint to Thakur Jeevan Singh ji that Lokram ji is violating the orders of the government. Thakur sent his soldiers for Lok ramji. Lok ram ji could sense what was wrong. So, he told soldiers that, "I am an old man. I will come slowly. You may go". In the time being, Lokram ji went to every body's house, who had auspicious occasions, and told them, "The soldiers had come and informed that, we may sing and dance". So by the time that he reached the court, there were many such houses, which started the rituals. When Thakur ji inquired that why did he violate the orders. Lok ram ji replied, "Thakur ji, you are mistaken. It is not only me who is doing that, but come with me to the terrace, I'll show you, how, all residents of Surajgarh are singing." Thakur ji smiled, as he knew he could not punish the whole village. Lokramji convinced the king that customs are essential part of the occasions in family and unavoidable in family at shekhawati, After this, Thakur ji attended the wedding of Lok ramji's son, Gajananada ji.

As told by the grand daughter of Lokramji, the handwritten Raksha yantra, katyayini Pooja vidhi, Mantras etc. could be found in the basket of his room for years.

Lok ram ji earned a lot during his tenure. He had- two havelis, 2 wells, 211 bigha agricultural land 5 camels, 15 cows and a horse. The author has witnessed the guns, barchi, bhala and sword, gifted by Thakur Jeevan Singh. Besides that, he was bestowed 111 bigha land in Mandawa by the ruler of Mandawa, Harisinghji. Lok ramji, got the well constructed on that land, because of which many families started living there and the place was famous as, "Loke ki Dhani". Out of 111 Bigha land, Lokramji donated 55bigha land to Kumhars, and allowed to drink water from well. Shyaochand Kumhar is the present holder of land.

Lok Ramji- Saviour of cows

In Vikram Samvat 1956, there was a draught. No food, No water. Despite draught, miraculously, both the wells of Lokramji were filled with water and everybody would get free water.

During the same time, muslims of Jhunjhunu, entrapped forty cows of Surajgarh, to slaughter them. Lok ram ji heard this and informed Thakur ji about this. But looking at the urgency of the situation, he could not wait. He confronted those muslims singlehandedly. Although he got injured during this, but he could stop them from taking away the cows, till Thakur ji came with the soldiers.

Thakur ji was happy with this and bestowed an honour upon Lokram ji. He was awarded a sword by Thakur ji. Even today there are scenes depicted on the walls of Jhunjhunu fort, to witness this.

Lok Ram ji and Ruler of Mandawa

Thakur Harisingh ji of Mandawa and Thakur of Surajgarh had close friendly relations. Harisinghji visited Surajgarh many times and one of his visits met Lok ram ji- Pandit and an astrologer. He consulted Lokram ji regarding the marriage proposal he received from Siraj Kanwar. But Lok ram ji advised Harisingh ji not to consider this proposal, as the horoscope of Siraj Kanwar indicated her early death. Since, Harisinghji was young; he ignored this advice and married Siraj Kanwar. As per the prediction of Lok ram ji, she passed away. That reminded Harisingh ji of Lok ramji and then he held him in high esteem.

He consulted Lokram ji once again for his second marriage, which Lok ram ji affirmed, and he had a long happy life and had four kids.

One day Hari Singh ji called for Lokram ji by sending his horses. He knew about his wisdom, foretelling as well as bravery and was aware that he had saved the cows. He bestowed 111 Bigha land in Mandawa upon Lokramji.

The area surrounding this land was named," Lok Ram ji ki Dhani". Lok ram ji got stepwell constructed there and two rooms adjacent to the well. This is still known as "Loke ka kua".Few people migrated there and started living there because of the availability of water and fertile soil. They used to work in the farms of Lokramji. Shyokarna Jats family is one of them.

Few more families moved in and people called this place" Loke ka Baas" and then "Loke ki Dhani".

Lokramji's Benevolance

Lokram ji was very benevolent. He believed in Daan-Punya. All throughout the year, he would donate something or the other to the needy. He would give away blankets to the needy in winter. In the summers, he would keep sacks of different grains with him and would donate it to the poor.

He would give away money to the poor, as and when they needed. He would never ask them to return the money. Whenever the debtor would feel comfortable, he would return the money but Lokram ji would never take the interest amount. Above all this, people had a belief that, whatever they did with money borrowed from Lokramji, the work would be successful.

The famous Chappaniya kaal (1899-1900) –Vikram Samvat 1956

Picture Reference 7: Chappaniya Kaal(the famous famine of 1896)

In 1896, the rainfall was less than the normal rainfalls. In 1897 the rains were sufficient but in the next year 1897-98, the rains were profuse, but again 1899 was a problem year. This was the worst year in which rainfall fell to 60-65%. The result was the famine, followed by epidemic, malaria & cholera and the famine was so severe that the tribals of Rajputana, Madhya Pradesh (central Provinces), Gujarat (Bombay Presidency), Hissar, Bhiwani, and other places died in thousands. The tragedy is still sung in the folk songs of these areas.

The famine relief in the British Provinces was organized by the Government of Lord Curzon and around 25% of the affected people were relieved as per the official figures, but the native princes of Rajputana and Gujarat who were autonomous failed to curb the death toll.

There was no water to drink. All the animals and people of the lower caste, who did not have access to stepwell water, were dying of thirst and hunger. The farmers and their cattle were dying. The water level of the well had gone deep down. It is irony that the water had become the most precious thing. The people who had relatives in Rajasthan were trying to reach out to them, with the help. The Marwari traders and industrialists, were willing to extend their help to the draught struck places, by donating huge amount of money. Shri Ram Kumar Ghagshyan lived in Calcutta. He collected the huge amount of funds from the Marwari seths of the region, as donations(in up and west bengal), for the people in Surajgarh. He returned to Surajgarh, but did not disburse the complete amount towards this cause, rather used the sum for the construction of huge haveli of two chowks.

"Nobody can Prosper with the misappropriated money for charity"

Hence the family of Ram Kumar Ghagshyan had to face the adverse consequences. Ram Kumar could not survive long after this. During the construction of haveli, few labors collapsed and died because of lack of food and water. The villagers connote this to the curse of the people who died. Nobody prospered in this haveli. Even today, haveli stands tall. Ram Kumar also offered some money from this fund to Lok ram ji 's family but they refused to accept that.

Lokram ji's virtue and his distinct qualities

Lokram ji was blessed with a son named "Gajananda" (Meaning Lord Ganesha). His son was equally benevolent and efficient in his work. He was well versed with the rites and rituals performed by Brahmins and highly educated in Sanskrit.

Despite of himself being Brahmin, Lokramji would never accept any "Dharma, Daan". He was so rigid that he would not allow, even a single seed of grain in the form of Daan. If anybody would insist on offering something, he would take it but would not keep it at home but would send it to Nohra and would give away this to Suja, a close disciple of Lokramji.

Pandit Lokram ji had four other siblings. They were all fair and believed in proper justice and hence they were considered Panch. They constructed the Panchon ka Kuva. Lokram ji was considered best Panch and people still remember that his "Lath"- Cane stick, was revered by the residents.

He adored his grandchildren- Srinivas ji, Rambilas ji and Godavari. He would honour her granddaughter as Devi roop. She used to talk a lot to his grandfather. In those days Lokram ji's health was ailing and hence Godavari would advise him to visit a doctor, rather than a Vaidhya. He portended correctly about his grandson, Rambilas ji. He said, "Don't consider, Rambilas as the simple man. He is very learned and has come from the town near Haridwar, which is Omkar nagari and the evidence of this is the mark of "Om" embossed on his body, since his birth. Lokramji, who also was the devotee of Sun, gave away his enlightenment to Rambilasji and advised him to follow the devotion to sun throughout his life time. Lok ram ji was learned and had good knowledge of Tantra and Mantra. He could even sense the "Upari Hawa", which is prevalent in Surajgarh. He would interact with the souls and Bhoot Pret. This is evident through an incident. Mahadev Pujari resided in the Ghagshyan ka mohalla near panchon ka Kuva. In the Pujari's family, three women died immediately after the marriage and it was prevalent that due to untimely death, they reached "Pret yoni" and hence became "Bhootani" in the well, constructed by Lokramji(Panchon ka Kuva). If any resident would go to the well, early in the morning, they could hear the sound of giggling and jumping into the water and hence, the women folk would be afraid to fetch water from the well. Lokramji's family also experienced this. But Lok ramji was never afraid off these Bhootanis, rather he would scold them, as if they were alive and they would go away. Till 1960, only Lokramji's family would be the first to fetch water from the well. Lok ram ji carried a cane-stick made of teak with the face of Lion made of silver, at one end and the sheet of silver at other end. He used this stick to shoo away the bhoot pret.

He foretold his death and described that he would die at 11'oclock on Kartik ekadashi in Vikram Samvat 1977. The family members need not to worry. He directed that his dead body should not be laid down on the floor; rather he got a bed constructed out of Peepal wood. He also directed to use only Chandan wood in his last rites. He passed away on the same day that he declared. Thakur BishanSingh ji attended his funeral.

Chapter 4

Parents of Shri Ram Bilas ji Ghagshyan

Points covered

- **Rambilasji's parents**
- **Wedding of Gajananda ji with Haripyari Devi**
- **Return of Gajanada ji from Calcutta**
- **Gajananda ji and Bavaliya Baba**
- **Impact of Partition and Independence of India**
- **Death of Gajananda ji**
- **Haripyari Devi: Mother of Rambilas ji**

Chapter 4

Parents of Shri Ram Bilas ji Ghagshyan

Father: GAJANANDJI GHAGSHYAN

Picture Reference 8: Gajananda ji Ghagshyan

Late Shri Gajananda Ji Ghagshyan was born to Lokramji & Gaura devi in year 1885, at Surajgarh. Gajananda ji was named so by his father Sh. Lokram Ji, very sensibly, for "Gajananda" means Great like elephant, Great Physique, bright eyes and physically strong. Moreover Gaura Devi was very affectionate towards her younger son, so means "Gauri Suta"- Son of Gaura Devi- beloved of mother as per Hindu mythology.

Gajananda ji's elder brother "Madhavaram" took only primary education and then took to farming and took care of farms and property of the father. He got married to Radha Janki Devi ji from Tiba Basai. They had no children so they adopted elder son of Gajananda ji, Srinivas ji. Srinivas ji got married to Gigi devi, grand daughter of Vishwanath ji Pansari and daughter of Munimji of Chirawa.

Gajananda ji had good command over Sanskrit and Mathematics. Although there was no schools, but Gurus at their Gurukuls imparted knowledge. Gajanandaji had taken formal education in Sanskrit, from Acharya Snehiram Shashn from Chirawa at Raibahadur Seth Suryamal Shivprasad Ved Vedang Sanskrit Mahavidyalaya. He took mathematics training from Ban Bhatt.

During his Sanskrit education, he came close to Pandit Ramji Lalji Shastri of Chirawa, who later became Principal of Sanskrit Mahavidyalaya. Pandit Ramji lalji Shastri was very learned and ardent Vaishnav, hence would not allow anybody to take his photograph. It was only on the insistence of Gajananda ji that he allowed himself to be photographed, but with the condition that he would keep his Thakur ji on his head.

Pandit Ramji lalji was the man who did Mahalaxmi Yajna for 64 days and Jugal Kishore Birla was bestowed the wealth. Jugal Kishore ji's business empire grew and he had JK synthetics, JK cement, JK Tyres, JK cotton Mills. He even made the kundli of Rambilas ji, Son of Gajananda ji.

GAJANANDA JI'S WEDDING AND QUEEN VICTORIA'S DEATH

Gajanand ji got married to HarPyari Devi of Chirawa on 2nd February 1901, Saturday. The Barat proceeded to Chirawa on 3rd February 1901, and stayed there for three days. Lok ram ji was very wise and intelligent. In 1901 AD, when Queen Victoria died on 22ndJanuary, the British ruled India and Surajgarh was under Jaipur Riyasat. So, British declared National Mourning till the cremation date of Queen Victoria and hence it was ordered that till Februry 4th, 1901 there should beno celebrations and no singing and dancing. The ruler of Jaipur Sawai Jai Singh announced this to be abided by all regions. The rulers of Shekhawati, including Surajgarh, were forced to follow the orders. Lok ramji's son Gajananda ji's wedding was scheduled during those five days only. As per the Marwadi rituals, they had to sing as Janau, Chak Bhaat, Tilak ceremonies were organized. This was audible to others and hence enviously, somebody complaint to Thakur Jeevan Singh ji that Lokram ji is violating the orders of the government. Thakur sent his soldiers for Lok ramji. Lok ram ji could sense what was wrong. So, he told soldiers that, "I am an old man. I will come slowly. You may go". In the time being, Lokram ji went to every body's house, which had auspicious occasions, and told them, "The soldiers had come and informed that, we may sing and dance". So by the time that he reached the court, there were many such houses, which started the rituals. When Thakur ji inquired that why did he violate the orders? Lok ram ji replied, "Thakur ji, you are mistaken. It is not only me who is doing that, but come with me to the terrace, I'll show you, how, all residents of Surajgarh are singing." Thakur ji smiled, as he knew he could not punish the whole village. After this, Thakur ji attended the wedding of Lok ramji's son, Gajananada ji. Since the father-in Law of Gajananda ji, Devi Sahay ji Sehal, and his brother-in Laws Tarachand ji & Isardasji, who were next to King of Khetri, there was a grand wedding and people bestowed the gifts and Jewellery upon the newly wedded couple.

Gajanada ji and Harpyari Devi had two sons and three daughters of which two daughters expired and only Godavari Devi could survive. His two sons were Srinivas ji and Ram Bilas ji.

Few months after marriage Gajananda ji went to Calcutta, for earning and he returned in 1912 to Surajgarh. Over and above being a good mathematician, he was also a very good astrologer and Pandit. Gajananda ji earned huge amount of money and brought it to Surajgarh. His father, Lokram ji got a well, two rooms and a hanuman temple constructed at Loke ka Baas. He even made arrangement for wooden bed in the rooms, so that passer by can take rest and can satiate their thirst. This step well is known as "Loke ka Kua", and the information is encrypted on the walls.

Gajanandji went back to Calcutta in 1914, and returned in early 1920, as Lokram ji was not keeping well.

Return of Gajananda ji from Calcutta

In year 1920, Gajanada ji came back to Surajgarh. It is said that he saved and accumulated twenty thousand silver coins from his hard work for twenty years of work. He returned from Calcutta to Delhi then Gurgaon then Narnaul via train and Lokramji sent two camels to Narnaul to fetch Gajanada ji back home to Surajgarh. On one camel, Gajanada himself rode and then on second he loaded two gunny bags containing silver coins and weighing hundred kilograms.

He had a very grand and warm welcome at Surajgarh. It is very famous, as in those days, only Rulers and Vaniks would have that much wealth and Brahmins would lead a humble life. So, it was one of its kind affairs, when a Brahmin, Gajanada ji, earned so much wealth. He brought pride to the family.

Security of the wealth

Since, earning tremendous wealth was one of its kind incidences, it spread throughout the village. Lokramji was concerned about the security of this wealth. So he called upon Chajju Chejara (Mason), and asked him to dig the earth in the corners of the rooms and under the staircase. They stored half the coins in the pot and they were buried in those dug out places and the colored stone slabs were kept on the dug places. The stone shelves were constructed above this. Around one fourth of the coins were put into the batuas, which were sealed. Rest of the one fourth was used for regular use. These batuas were then kept in the niches in the wall and was covered by the family members with brick and cement and to mark the place wooden keg was put there.

Life after return to Surajgarh

Gajanada ji's first daughter Narmada died at the age of one, due to high fever. The second daughter Godavari also passed away the same day as her elder sister Narmada. This incident had a deep impact on Ghagshyan's family and they were deeply mourned. It also affected Lokramji's health adversely.

Gajananda ji, who was in Calcutta, prayed to Goddess KSatyayini and urged her to bless him with a daughter. Katyayini Devi (The Godess) came into Gajanada ji's dream and affirmed his prayer. After which, he went to meet his family in Surajgarh. His dream come true, when his third daughter was born, and they named her also Godavari. Godavari was very close to Lokramji. Lokram ji used to bless her and would consider her incarnation of Goddess Durga. In those days women did not interact with the males of the family also. But Godavari Devi, talked to her grandfather Lokram ji and would always show her concern towards Lokramji's deteriorating health and would always warn him not to take the treatment of Chotelal ji vaidya ji, rather consult a good doctor, so that he recuperates. But the health of Lokramji was deteriorating.

Gajanada ji as Money lender (Mahajan)

Gajanada ji, who had earned 20,000 silver coins in his service at Calcutta, started the Money lending. He would provide loan on interest, to people in need. His wife HarPyari Devi was very strict in the terms and condition of the lending. She would make sure about the interest rate, period of repayment and Guarantor and would even take the thumb impression of the debtor. This business flourished for thiry years. The Principal amount remains intact and the income from the interest was enough to handle the daily expenses. He also had a farm, which would be cultivated by contract farmers in the ratio of 40:60, where 40% would be the share of farmers and rest would remain with Gajanand ji. This was enough for the annual consumption. He would barter the grains to get other grains from the other farmers. Between 1940 and 1949, Gajanada ji took his wife for the pilgrimage to Haridwar, Triveni and Ganga Sagar and Char Dham Yatra, whose records were verified by his grandson Savita prakash Sharma, to their visit to Badri-Kedar in 2009-10 and a copy of the records was confirmed by the religious historians who keep data of the family generation wise.

Gajananda ji and Bavaliya Baba

Gajanada ji had a good rapport with Bavaliya baba of Chirawa and would often visit him. When Lokramji was on death bed, Gajanand ji's friends- Bavaliya Baba, Pandit Ramji lal ji Shastri and Bassesar lal ji Tibrewala (Grandfather of Jagdish Tibrewala, Ahmedabad), visited Gajanadaji's house.

Bavaliya Baba, on meeting Lokramji, could make out that Lokram ji was Siddh yogi and Devotee of Goddess Durga, so Bavlaiya Baba, seek the blessings of Lokramji. Lokramji urged Bavaliya Baba to take care of his son Gajanada ji, after his death. Bavaliya baba assured Lokramji to take care of his son, and said, "Don't worry mata ji would take care of Gajanada."

He foretold his death and described that he would die at 11'oclock on Kartik ekadashi in Vikram Samvat 1977. The family members need not to worry. He directed that his dead body should not be laid down on the floor; rather he got a bed constructed out of Peepal wood. He also directed to use only Sandalwood in his last rites and dispose -off his ashes in Har ki Pedi. He passed away on the same day that he declared in year 1926. Thakur BishanSingh ji attended his funeral.

Before his death, Lokram ji preached to Gajanada ji, "To keep away non veg and wine from their house, as it is abode of God. Not to take "Sidha" (Eatables given to Brahmins) from anybody. Not to allow anybody with bad habits to enter the house. Take proper care of wealth and use it wisely."

The Ghagshyan clan still follows these preachings.

Gajanada ji's honor to Bawaliya Baba

He often used to visit Bawalia baba. Once on some good occasion, Gajanandji visited Bawaliya Baba- and said "Baba, mere ghar main thari kripa se shub karya ho rahio hain, en liye thane main yooh dhushalo odhano chahu hoon. Bawaliya Baba happily took it on shoulder and immediately, honoured Gajanandji with that dushala saying. Gajanand yo dushalo jad tak hain tere kade koi cheej ki kami koni pade. And blessed Gajanandji by saying brahmana ke chandi ka sikka kothaliya main dekha hoga, tere anaj ki boriyan bhar ke chandi ka sikka kamai hove gi." This came true for Gajananda ji. When he returned from Calcutta, after job, he had two gunny bags full of silver coins.

Gajananda ji and Bavaliya Baba's visit to Nawalgarh-witnessing the miracle-1

Once bavaliya Baba said to Gajananda ji and Ramji lalji Shastri," Let us go to Nawalgarh & meet mavdi (Bavaliya baba addressed her mother as Mavdi)." So all three went to Nawalgarh and visited Bavaliya Baba's house.

Bavaliya Baba's wife greeted three of them and then complaining to her husband said," You have renunciated and become saint, leaving behind the whole family to be fed. I have no livelihood. Its difficult for me to fulfil the basic requirements of the family."

Hearing this, Bavaliya Baba said, "How innocent and naive are you? Having said that, he sat down on the ground, and started rubbing the sand on ground with palm and fingers. To the utter surprise of everyone, the silver coins started to fell. Gajanada ji counted them as 42 silvercoins.

Bavaliya baba gave those coins to his wife and then returned to Chirawa. Ramji lalji and Gajanand ji bowed to Baba's Miracle.

Bavaliya Baba's Miracle witnessed by Gajananda ji

Once Gajananda ji visited Bavaliya baba at Chirawa. On the way, he thought of buying some fruits, Peda and Kanji Ka wada for Babaji. While the packaging of all these, he requested shopkeeper to pack two Pedas separately for himself and kept them in the other pocket of Kurta. When he reached Bavaliya Baba's place, he offered all the things that he had brought for him. Bvaliya Baba asked Gajananda ji to unpack all the things and distribute amongst seven people including Babaji and Gajanada ji. Gajananda ji divided all the things among all, including him. Everybody got 2 pieces each of every item. Bavaliya Baba, immediately enquired, "Why are you taking two Pedas, when you already have two in the right pocket of your Kurta?" Everybody was surprised to hear this, as nobody knew about those separately packed Pedas, except Shopkeeper and Gajannada ji.

Gajananda ji immediately realized that he was exposed to the great saint, who had enlightenment. He stood up and touched Babaji's feet.

Gajanadaji's Jhanki similar to Ganesh Narayanji's Jhanki

There was a huge procession of Gajananda ji's Jhanki. It was just like a chariot. He was wearing a shawl and a Head gear, similar to Ganesh Narayan ji and everybody in Chirawa mistook him as Bawaliya Baba only. He was reciting the devi mantra given to him by Ganesh Narayan ji. He got reverence as high as Bawaliya Baba, which was nothing but the miracle of the Bawaliya Baba.

Impact of partition and independence of India on Gajanada ji

By the year 1944-45, Gajanadaji and HarPyari Devi was a satisfied couple, having successfully fulfilled all their obligations towards their children and the family. Rambilasji was settled in Okara, Lahore(Now in Pakistan) and Srinivas ji was settled in Calcutta. Gajanada ji was extremely upset during the partition phase of 1946-48, when Bharat was divided into India and Pakistan. Rambilas ji and his sister Godavari Devi were in Okara at the time of partition and had sent their families back to Surajgarh in 1946. This was a traumatic incident for the family as Rambilasji and His Brother-in-law, had to leave everything behind and had to bear the brunt of partition. They faced lot of difficulties and family prayed for their safe return. By God's grace, both the families were hale and hearty, without any casualty. (THE DETAILS WOULD BE DEALT IN RAMBILASJI CHAPTER AT OKARA)

Grand marriage in the history of Ghagshyans

In 1948, Gajananda ji, married his granddaughter Bhagwati, daughter of Srinivasji, in the Bheda family of Chirawa. It was a grand marriage. In those days groom on elephant and Baratis on camels was the sign of affluence and this came true in Bhagwati's marriage. Rambilasji spent Rs. 10,000 in that Wedding. The people from those days, still talk about this in Surajgarh and chirawa. The marriage has enhanced the reputation of the Bhedas in Chirawa. Gajananda ji was upset after the wedding, as Rambilas ji spent huge amount in this wedding, despite the fact that he was not settled after returning from Okara. Then, Rambilasji went to Calcutta but Rambilas ji did not send money order for six months, which otherwise he regularly sent from wherever he worked earlier. Gajnanada ji was worried and decided to go to Calcutta to look into the matter. After reaching Calcutta, Rambilasji discussed with him about his employement. He had ventured in the Bangle industry, in partnership with Agarwal (Halwai) from Pilani. They were into the manufacturing of Bangles. But looking into the account books, gave the right picture to Gajanada ji and he could make out that the business was into losses. Rambilas ji had invested all his money into this venture but was realized by Gajanand ji that his partner cheated him, since Rambilas ji was a non-commercial business man. Gajanand ji, settled the accounts and ordered Rambilas ji to return to Surajgarh with Gajanand ji.

Death of Gajanandji

In the year 1950, Gajanadaji was not keeping well and had breathing problem which was diagnosed as infection in the lungs. Chotelal ji Vaidya ji was giving him the medicines. There were no doctors in Surajgarh. Chotelal ji Vaidya ji realized that there had been water retention in the lungs and ribs of Gajananda ji and he extracted out that water twice, but Gajananda ji survived for 15 days only after that.

Mother

Picture Reference 9: Rambilasji's Mother, Harpyari Devi

Harpyari devi was the mother of Shri Ram bilas ji Ghagshyan. She was born in 1887, at Chirawa to Devi Sahay Sehal. Sehal's were affluent in those days. She was a religious and pious lady. She did Chandrayani vrat (Fasting without food only on water for three months) many a times during her life time because of which she was worshipped by the villagers. She was commanding, strong willed and born manager. Her two brothers Isardas ji and Tarachand ji Sehal were tehsildar in the Khetri Darbar and hence were considered to be very powerful and influential people. Harpyari Devi had acquired these traits from her brothers. She had good controlling skill, which helped her to manage the huge Ghagshyan family. She had commanding voice and if anybody dare to cross through her farm, she would yell at him. No passer-by would dare to stop by the farm. Besides that she would not allow any male other than the family, to enter the house beyond "poli".Her mother was the pious lady and was firm believer of the rituals, which Har Pyari devi had imbibed.

Padmshree Late Sisram Ola's Memories About Haripyari Devi

As had been narrated by, Late Shri Sis Ram ji Ola (Cabinet Minister in Indian Government), "We would go to headmasterji's house(Rambilas ji), to take free lessons from him. But, if maa(Harpyari Devi), would be around, everybody would sit on the floor. Nobody dare to sit on chair or bed. This was the awe and reverence that all of us had towards her."

She was a good fund manager, which is reflected in the fact that she did not devaluate the earned money of her husband Gajananda ji. Gajananda ji earned 20,000 silver coins and came back to Surajgarh. HarPyari devi, managed this fund throughout her life and used this for Mahajani purpose and hence could multiply that money. This also shows her intellectual capabilities, which she had conferred to her son, Ram Bilas ji. People of the village and other relatives would seek her advice before taking up any task.

PART III

RAMBILAS JI'S LIFE

Chapter 5

Rambilas Ji's Birth and His Childhood

Points covered

- **Birth of Rambilasji**
- **Early Education**
- **Environment of Chirawa**
- **Impact of Maternal grandparents**

Chapter 5

Rambilas Ji's Birth and His Childhood

Birth of Rambilas ji

Shri Rambilas ji was one of the three children of Gajananda ji Ghagshyan. Rambilas ji's elder brother was Srinivas ji and the younger sister was Godavari. He was born to Gajanada ji and Harpyari devi on 13th May 1913 at Surajgarh.

Lokramji, Rambilasji's grandfather portended correctly about his grandson, Rambilas ji. He said, "Don't consider, Rambilas as the ordinary / simple man. He is very learned and has come from the town near Haridwar, (kashi) which is Omkar nagari and the evidence of this is the mark of "Om" embossed on his body, since his birth." Lokramji, who also was the devotee of Sun, gave away his enlightenment to Rambilasji and advised him to follow the devotion to sun throughout his life time.

Pandit Ramjilal shastri, friend of Gajanada ji, in discussion with Lokramji, made Rambilas ji's Kundali, and advised that his name must have a prefix-"Ram", as the kundali exhibits the characteristics similar to Lord Rama. He listed the following characteristics: obedient to Parents, Intellectual, chivalorious, helpful to siblings, well-mannered, decent, believer in Lord Shiva. This was coincidental that later Rambilasji married Janaki devi and Lord Rama's wife was also Janaki (Sita).

Early Education

Before joining the formal schooling, Rambilasji was taught by his learned grandfather and father. His grandfather Lokramji taught him Sanskrit. Gajanada ji, Rambilasji's father who himself learnt Mathematics form Ban Bhatt, taught him Mathematics. For quick calculations one required a lot of practise and one had to learn counts or pahadas – as they were called. whe Rambilas was young he was taught counts up to 40. He was also taught- “Savaiya”, “Dyodha”, “Hoontas”, “Dhonchas”, and “Poonchas”. this refers to the results when a number is multiplied by 1, ½, 2/4, ¾, 4/4 and 5/4 times. In those days when calculating machines and computers were unknown. The family members could sense yearn to learn more in Rambilasji and hence, decided to send him for formal schooling to his maternal uncle at CHIRAWA.

Chirawa Days- 1920-Mahadev Somani School, Rambilas ji and Sh. Panna lal Kaushik

Picture Reference 10: Mahadeo Somany School, Chirawa

Rambilas ji took his primary and middle education at Mahadev Somany School, Chirawa. Shri Pandey Ji was his teacher at that time. Another friend of Rambilas ji, who studied in the same class was Panna lal ji Kaushik. They were very close friends, as they had much in common like the natives of their forefathers. He was not financially sound, but was keen to learn. Rambilas ji's grandfather (Nana) and Mama were well-off and had huge haveli at Chirawa, but Rambilas ji never showed off and would be self-motivated to learn.

Rambilas ji and Panna lal ji used to go to Pandeyji's haveli near police station to study and practice Mathematics, for free. Panna lalji studied till standard 8th and both Ram bilas ji and Pannalalji cleared the board exams of Class 5 & 8 together. Rambilas ji continued his studies.

Later Panna lal became a well- known face of Shekhawati. He was the first Brahmin of Surajgarh(Sehi) to become the Director at Birla Mills. He became so popular that Sh. Jawahar lal Nehru, asked him to contest election from Jaipur in the first elections in 1951-52 and he won and became MP. Panna Lal Kaushik died in a plane crash in 1953. The story about his loyality towards birlas was exemplary. Very few people know that, during the last flight he was boarding, he was carrying some important and confidential documents of birla,

In the aircraft, when the pilot crew announced that there was a major fault and the aircraft had caught fire. Upon learning this, Pannalalji Kaushik was the first to jump from the aircraft – and the intention was so clear that – even if life goes, the important document should be safe. Unfortunately the parachute did not open upon jumping and hedied, and some of the survivors narrated this story.

Environment of Chirawa and freedom struggle– 1920

shekhawati architecture marvel - a kua at chirawa

Picture Reference 11: Chirawa in 1920

Rambilasji Sharma and Freedom struggle movement-1920-1930

This was the time when the Civil Disobedience Movement was at its high. But due to the samantshahi neeti of land lords, the public was terrified and was afraid to even discuss then politic situation and hence were kept away from the Indian freedom struggle. The teachers were appointed by the British. Mostly the teachers from UP and Punjab were deputed to the schools in Shekhawati region. Principal of Chirawa high school, Shri Pyare Lal ji gupta, Shri Manmohan nathji Jutshi, Principal Pilani High School and Shri Radhey Shyam Misra, Principal Nawalgarh, Thakur Narayan Singh and Dr. Gulzari Lal ji Dikhshit etc. participated in the Indian freedom struggle but secretly as this was against the orders of Land lords of those days. Indian freedom Movement started to strengthen its hold in Shekhawati Region. Because of this, the public awareness towards freedom struggle increased and hence the teachers had to bear the brunt, as they were secretly increasing this awareness amongst the masses. In light of this Shri Pyare lal ji was expelled from Chirawa High School. The scouts who would volunteer in the fairs in villages would revolt against the exploitation of labor by the land lords.

When Lokmanya Gangadhar Tilak died on 1st August 1920, his funeral procession was done at Mumbai. But when the news travelled to Chirawa, students in Chirawa High School came out of the classes and gathered at "Shree Krishna Vachanalaya" to hold a condolence meeting under the leadership of Shri Ramji Lalji. But the tehsildar of Chirawa informed this to the ruler of Khetri, who showed his disapproval to this.

The terrifying environment of Chirawa was witnessed by Rambilas ji also, as he was studying in Chirawa and staying at his mama's place. Since, Rambilas ji was also not allowed to participate in any activity related to freedom struggle by his mama, he would go to his teacher's haveli, in precinct to study, but actually he would use that time, away from mama's house to connect to freedom movement.

To help the people participating in freedom struggle, he would give the prior information of any action planned against them by the ruler of Khetri, as he could get to know about this from his mama. This was how he contributed to the cause of freedom.

Impact of nana, mama and mother on Rambilasji's Personality

Isardas ji Sehal and Tara chand ji, mama of Rambilasji, were Tehsildar under the aegies of ruler of Khetri. They had to handle land and revenue administration. Because of this the discussions regarding the administration of Khetri tehsil, were common in the household. Since, they were at the higher designation; people of higher stature would visit them. This exposed Rambilasji to the nitty gritties of administrative skills, which he could utilize later in his career.

His mother nurtured him with religious values and made him family oriented person. He observed the management skills of his mother and imbibed them.

Books that Rambilas ji read

- **Vivekananda**
- **Shakespeare**
- **Premchand Munshi**

Rambilasji's friends

- Saligram gupta
- Matadin bhageria-freedom fighter
- Gilluram bharatia-secretary pb high school
- Mahavirprasad vaid-mgr at birla)
- Himmatramka
- Banvarilal mishra "Kavi Suman"
- Pt. Jhabbarmal Sharma-jasrapur,(journalist)
- Hajarilalji Sharma-MLA
- Pannalal kaushik
- Narrotamlal joshi (friend and relative)
- Bajaranglal Somani
- Pt. Pyralal Gupta
- Banvarilal Dungerka
- Dungermal gupta

Chapter 6

Early Life

Points covered

- **Indian freedom struggle**
- **Rambilasji's wedding**
- **Rambilasji's wife**

Chapter 6

Early Life

Indian freedom struggle and Rambilasji's role in it

Since, the ruler of Khetri was in favour of British, he did not want his confidante's to participate in Indian freedom struggle and invite the anger of British. Rambilasji's mama, being the tehsildar at Khetri Riyasat, followed the dictum and announced that nobody from their family should engage in the activities against British. So, Rambilas ji was strictly not allowed to participate in any andolan. Once he was spotted with some of the students who were carrying out agitation against the Britishers, the tehsildar of Chirawa, who was his mama, caught him in that procession and complained about this to his nana that Haripyaribai(Rambilasji's mother) has sent Rambilas toChirawa for better studies and not to become a Gandhian and that was the time he could not directly participate in the freedom struggle, but he quietly continued supporting freedom movement by supporting his fellow freedom fighter, he would do any documentation in English and hindi, passing of information. One of his friend name Kavi Banvarilal suman used to write patriotic poems and make copies of it to distribute it to all in the school and college, and if some body would ask for it they said, the teacher has asked to recite it and speak in the class tomorrow.

Another friend was Banvrilal mishra-Pistoli, actually Banvarilal was very fearless and used to carry a pistol will him 24 hours, and hence his identity was pistol, so he was nicknamed –Pistoli.

Matadin Bhageria and Gilluram Bhartia were another persons in their group during chirawa days.

A few collegetime friends of Headmasterji became teacher even before Headmasterji, and during freedom struggle, they would allow students to participate in agitation against britishers and upon questioning would name student leader responsible. The fact of the matter was they would themselves plan it all. Once they were caught during civil disobedient movents and were sent to jail- along with Headmasterji, and Isardasji Sahal helped them to get released. in lie of 5 KODO ki maar for each one.

Rambilas ji's wedding-1929

Isardas ji who was tehsildar of Chirawa, would have to screen the goods, coming to Chirawa, or Going towards Khetri, Surajgarh etc, at check post of Chirawa. He would never take anything from the goods and would perform his duty righteously. So, Rungta's of Bagad, whose goods were also scanned at Chirawa Check Post, got impressed with Isardasji and built a good rapport with him and so would often discuss even family matters. One day, in discussion with Rungta Seth, he mentioned about his nephew, Rambilasji, who had passed intermediate with first Division and was of marriageable age. Immediately, Rungta Seth, gave him the reference of Devki nandan ji Chomal's younger daughter, Janaki devi, who had passed class 8 exams, which was a big achievement for girls in those days. Since, Devki nandan ji and his wife passed away many years ago, Rungta Seth, informed about this matrimonial match to Shiv Kumar ji Chomal, son of Devki nandan ji. Shiv Kumar Ji, immediately sent a "Nai", with the proposal to Ghagshyans in Surajgarh. Rambilasji's father Gajananda ji and Mama Isardas ji called Ramji lal ji shastri and discussed about the proposal for Rambilas ji. Ramji Lal ji talked to his friend Murari lal ji Mishra of Bagad, about this. Murari Lal ji seconded this proposal as the Chomal family was one of the affluent and influential family of Bagad. Devki nandan ji's son, Shivkumar ji Chomal was very famous and close to the Rungta seths. Shiv Kumar Ji Chomal, then went to Surajgarh, to meet Gajanada ji, and gave affirmation from their side and invited them to visitBagar to see Janaki

Gajanandji's wisdom in selecting appropriate match for his son Rambilasji.

Gajanandji went to see Jankidevi at Baggar along with his friends, his Brother-in Law- Isardasji Sahal, one friend and Murarilal Mishra.

There he asked Janaki only one question-"Beti, if lot of guest suddenly come to our house and you don't have sufficient stock of fresh vegetables, how would you manage? What would you do?"

She replied, "I will consult my mother in law. I will use the dry stock of mangodi, papad, sangaria, to prepare delicious food, use curd for preparing kadhi, will make nice rotis and serve with homemade butter."

Gajanandji was very happy with reply and immediately affirmed that Janaki would be perfectmatch for Rambilasand she wouldenhance reputation of our family for sure.

As Rambilas ji spent most of his time at his nana's place in Chirawa, they insisted to carry out all the marriage rituals from Chirawa itself. So, his Janau, Tilak, baan etc. were organized in Chirawa.

The wedding was decided and whole Bagad was decorated. Haveli and school of Rungta's were booked for three days, as in those days Baraat stayed for 2-3 days.

Rambilasji's reluctance to marriage

Although in those times, early marriages were prevalent and boys also got married between 12-15years of age. But even after his marriage, Rambilas ji would always complaint to his mother, "Why did you marry me, so early? I wanted to study." His mother would always tell her, "This is the trend. Boys get married by age of 15."

Rambilasji's Wife: Janaki Devi Devisahay Chomal(Bagar)

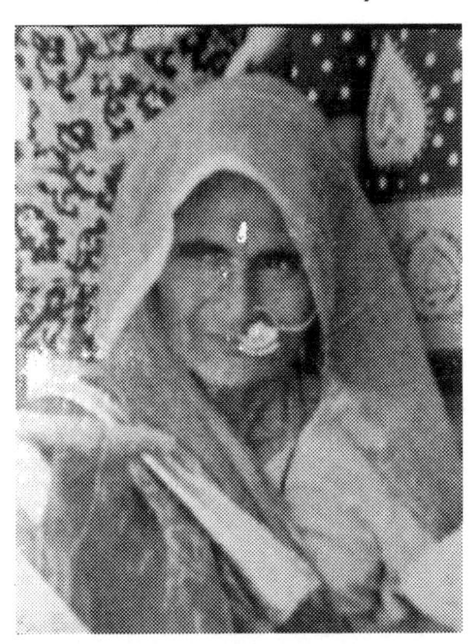

Picture Reference 12: Janaki Devi, Wife Of Rambilasji

Picture Reference 13: Shiv Kumar Chomal, Rambilasji's Brother in Law

Janaki Devi ji was the youngest daughter of Devki nandan ji Chomal of Bagad. The Chomal family was one of the affluent and influential family of Bagad. Janakidevi's brother Shiv kumar ji was very famous and close to Rungtas. Her parents passed away at the early age, when she was just 5. So she was brought up by his elder brother. She being orphaned at early age was a quiet child and would just follow the directions of the elders in the family. She studied till class 8th. She was very dear to her elder brother, Shiv Kumar ji. After her wedding, her life at Surajgarh, remained confined to taking orders. She was very religious and pious lady and worshipped Thakur ji and Tulsi mata. She would light diya under peepal tree, every Saturday. She had a routine of offering Roti to cows. She was the only lady in the whole family who would go to temple. She was a good cook and people relished the dishes prepared by her. She used to cook Sangri ka Saag, Mangodi ki Kadhi, Gajre ki kadhi, Keri ki lunggi, Baingan ka Sabji. She devoted her whole life in taking care of her mother-in-law, who was a strict disciplinarian. Janaki Devi had no courage to speak to her mother-in-law.

Chapter 7

Higher Education and Early career

Points to be covered

- **First graduate of Surajgarh**
- **Teaching at School of Bissau**
- **Post Graduation from Lahore**
- **As teacher at Chirawa High School**

Chapter 7

Higher Education and Early career

1932-1934
RAMBILASJI AND THE HONOUR TO BE FIRST GRADUATE OF SURAJGARH

सूरजगढ़

प्रत्याशी– 10, वोट– 2,26,442

जानें सूरजगढ़ को

'कैसल ऑफ द सन' यानि सूरज का किला कहलाता है सूरजगढ़। केडिया फैमिलीज का होम टाउन, जो देश की टॉप इंडस्ट्रीयल फैमिलीज में से है। मंडी, लाख बैंगल्स और फोर्ट के लिए प्रसिद्ध। यहां के पहले ग्रेजुएट शख्स थे स्व. रामबिलास शर्मा, जो हैडमास्टरजी के नाम से प्रसिद्ध थे, उन्होंने लाहौर यूनिवर्सिटी से ग्रेजुएशन किया था। हरियाणा से टच में होने के कारण यहां राजस्थानी और हरियाणवी मिक्स कल्चर एक अलग टेस्ट देता है। यहां के लोगों की खूबी है यारों के यार हैं तो दुश्मनों के दुश्मन नंबर वन।

मतदाता

भाजपा–कांग्रेस में टक्कर?

श्रवण कुमार

संतोष अहलावत

newspaper name- Dainik Amber,
dt.01 december 2013, Sunday
published fr dundlod(Jhunjhunu)
column:Aapni Shekhawati, page no-10.
Late.Rambilasji sharma-headmasterji's name
still remembered in history of surajgarh
matter underlined with blue pen.

Picture Reference 14: Newspaper clipping mentioning Rambilasji as the first graduate of Surajgarh

Rambilas ji was the first graduate of Surajgarh in the year 1932. Thakur Raghubir Singh, publicly honoured Rambilas ji for his achievement, in his palace, in the presence of dignitaries. Raghubir Singhji was the king of Bissau and Surajgarh jointly. He requested Rambilas ji to teach English at school in Bissau. Headmasterji taught there for two years. In those days teachers and the Principals in Shekhawati region were from Punjab and Uttar Pradesh. Rambilasji's literacy mission started from Bissau. But then he requested Thakur Raghubir Singh to allow him to go to Lahore, to earn higher degree.

Picture Reference 15: Headmasterji and Raja Raghubir Singh, King of Bissau &Surajgarh

1934-36

Picture Reference 16: Governament College, Lahore

The British Government, after the annexation of Punjab - the last area to be conquered and brought under the Crown - felt that they had to demonstrate their might to the hard fighting Sikhs. So, they did everything on a grand scale here to establish the prestige of the conquering Imperial Government. Besides establishing a magnificent Government College at Lahore, many other institutions had been set up through the government's initiative in Lahore even before they were established in Delhi. So, Lahore was the education hub of those times.

Rambilasji moved to Lahore for Post-Graduation at Government College of Lahore. It was one of the best educational institutions of those times. The two years were the turning point in Rambilasji's life. He got better exposure and also started thinking beyond the boundaries of Shekhawati. He had an honor of being first Post Graduate of Surajgarh from Lahore University. Shri Lal Krishna Advani was also the graduate of Government College Lahore and because of this;during one of the visit in 1956-57 in PB high school, Surajgarh, jhunjhunu,(he had affinity for Rambilas ji when rambilasji told him that he postgrduated from Lahore university and that he is the principal of the high school) and wanted him to work for RSS later, when Advani ji was working to establish RSS in Shekhawati between 1955-65. More of the details are not available with the author about who were the people in Lahore, upon research it was known that Lala Lajpat Rai was actively engaged in freedom struggle in Pakistan occupied Punjab.

1936- 1941- Chirawa High School

Rambilasji returned to Surajgarh in 1936. The same year his eldest son, Sh. Omprakash ji was born. Rambilas ji joined Chirawa high school as a teacher. He had good command over English, because of his education from the best institutes. He had charismatic voice. In those days GD Birla, had a discussion with his father in law, Mahadeo ji Somany, emphasizing on the need of strengthening English of the people of Shekhawati. The school annual function was organized to encourage the students and boost their potential. The educational leaders and the Industrialists were invited as the Chief Guest and the Guest of Honor. This was one of occasion where the students' performance could bring name, fame and reputation to the school and hence would increase the employability of the children. As a coordinator, Rambilas ji got the opportunity to address the students in one of these functions, where he chooses to speak in English. The chief guest was Sh. GD Birla, who was impressed to hear the speech of Rambilas ji and congratulated him for that. This was the first occasion when Rambilasji met GD Birla.

Chapter 8

Life at Okara

Points to be covered

- **About Okara**
- **Life at Sutluj Cotton Mills**
- **The strike and Sardar Patel**
- **The partition talks**
- **Sending family back to Surajgarh**

Chapter 8

Life at Okara

About Okara

Okara District is a district of **Lahore Division** of Punjab, Pakistan. The Multan Road connects the district capital, Okara withLcahore 110 km away. Okara began as a small town about 40 km from the city of Sahiwal. It later became a city in its own right. According to the 1998 census, the district had a population of 2,232,992 of which 12.84% were urban. The postal code of Okara is 56300.

Okara region was agricultural region with forests during the Indus Valley Civilization. The Vedic period is characterized by Indo-Aryan culture that invaded from Central Asia and settled in Punjab region. The Kambojas, Daradas, Kaikayas, Madras, Pauravas, Yaudheyas, Malavas, Saindhavasand Kurus invaded, settled and ruled ancient Punjab region. After overunning the Achaemenid Empire in 331 BCE, Alexander marched into present-day Punjab region with an army of 50,000. The Okara was ruled by Maurya Empire, Indo-Greek kingdom, Kushan Empire, Gupta Empire, White Huns, Kushano-Hephthalites and Shahi kingdoms.

In 997 CE, Sultan Mahmud Ghaznavi, took over the Ghaznavid dynasty empire established by his father, Sultan Sebuktegin, In 1005 he conquered the Shahis in Kabul in 1005, and followed it by the conquests of northern Punjab region. The Delhi Sultanate and later Mughal Empire ruled the region. The Punjab region became predominantly Muslim due to missionary Sufi saints whosedargahs dot the landscape of Punjab region.

After the decline of the Mughal Empire, the Sikh invaded and occupied Sahiwal. The Muslims faced severe restrictions during the Sikh rule. During the period of British rule there was a forest of Okaan where the city has been built. The city is a relatively new agricultural city. The word Okara for this district was actually originated from word Okan(A lush green tree with needle like leaves). The tree Okan gave birth to word Okanwali(Land of Okan) which ultimately finalized into Okara. During British rule the area was part of Montgomery District and contained a large saltpeterrefinery. At partition one of the two textile mills that Pakistan got was the one at Okara. The mill was known as Sutlej textile mill and belonged to Aditya Birla Group. It was Asia's biggest textile mill at that time. In 1982 the city became the headquarters of the newly created Okara District. Okara has had a railway line since 1892.

Okara District was previously part of Montgomery District which included Pakpattan, Sahiwal, Okara, districts, of Punjab. The predominantly Muslim population supported Muslim League andPakistan Movement. After the independence of Pakistan in 1947, the minority Hindus and Sikhs migrated to India while the Muslim refugees from India settled in the Okara district. Babu Rajab Alithe great Kavishari (a genre of Punjabi traditional poem) writer also belonged to this district.

Life at Sutluj Cotton Mills

Originally, SIL was set up with a composite textile mill at Okara (now in Pakistan) in 1934-37 by GD Birla.

The mills had installed capacity of 78000 spindles and 3000 looms. It had all departments including ginning, spinning, weaving, processing and printing, although printing of textiles was in its initial stage in those days. Over and above that a large no of cottage industries were there in Okara, still the demand of cloth could not be met. The basic reason for this was availability of the raw material.

G.D. purchased Kesoram cotton mills Calcutta and Hindustan times in Delhi and established Birla cotton mills in Okara Lahore in 1937 and named it Satluj cotton mills ltd(the largest cotton mills in South East Asia in those times).The civil construction work took around 3 years, and by 1940, the shades of the mills were ready, the officers colony along with swimming pool, independent 12 -15 bunglows with cemented road in the middle, proper plantation was done. A new unit has to be erected and idea was to have a modern textile units, first of its kind, hence first officers were appointed in the Satluj Cotton Mills, then they were given training daily in accordance to theirarea of handling. These officers were in turn asked to train the workers in respective departments. It was madea rule that no person will be appointed without proper training. All the machines were purchased from M/s Rieters, Switzerland, a company renowned for high quality of textiles machines. Once the machines arrived at Okarra, the entire erection was done by Indian mechanics under the guidance of experts from Rieters, Switzerland in year 1940.

On 20 May 1943 the Sutlej Cotton Mills, Okara, consigned 15 bales of cotton dhotis from Okara to Delhi and sent the railway receipt to Messrs. Jallan and Sons, Limited, Delhi, duly endorsed in their favour. THE railway receipt was presented by Messrs. Jallan and Sons, Limited, to the railway at Delhi on 22nd and 23 June 1948 and they were given delivery of 1676 pairs of dhotis. The rest of the consignment, consisting of 725 pairs of dhotis, had got damaged during, transit and accordingly Messrs. Jallan and Sons, Limited, refused to accept them. Correspondence ensued between Messrs. Jallan and Sons, Limited, on the one side and the railway on the other side resulting in a notice under Section 80, Civil P.C. by Messrs. Jallan and Sons, Limited, Delhi, upon the appropriate railway authority. The suit out of which the present proceedings have arisen was instituted on 8th May 1944 for recovery of Rs. 7,500 on account of depredation and damages.

They also started a private school – Birla School, in Okarra. This private school was originally known as Birla High School and was run by the management of SutlejCotton Mills, Okara.

Shri Mahavir Prasad ji Noondhwala,(resident of Pilani) brother in law of Rambilasji, got job at Sutluj Cotton Mills, Okara, Lahore as incharge of the dairy and canteen.

Mr Rajgarhia was manager in the mills. In discussion with GD Birla, he mentioned about Rambilasji, who was then working at Chirawa High School. Rambilas ji's mention immediately reminded him of the Chirawa high School's function in 1940, in which Rambilasji's speech was appreciated by all and he suggested Shri Mahaveer Prasad ji, to call Rambilas ji and appoint him as a teacher at Birla School, Okara. When Mahaveer Prasad ji went to Pilani, he called for Rambilas ji and discussed about the opportunity at Okara. Rambilasji was little reluctant to move to Okara, as he wanted to serve Shekhawati, but then Mahaveer Prasad ji, fixed the meeting of Rambilas ji with GD Birla, who was in Pilani at that time. GD Birla discussed with Rambilasji and could convince him to relocate to Okara.

GD Birla was so happy with the work and dedication of Rambilas ji that he promoted Rambilas ji as Principal of the school within six months at Okara. After which, the management allotted him an independent Bunglow.

Sir Datar Singh, Vice-Chairman, ICAR, maternal grandfather of Maneka Gandhi, was a big landlord. Dr G.S. Cheema, fruit adviser to the Government of India, had farms there. Baba Gurmukh Singh (G.S. Autos) had now settled at Burewala were among prominent people of Okarra and Rambilas Sharma had good terms with these people.

Okara had few industries upto 1950s, and a Military Dairy Farm in cantonment area. Rambilasji loved Okara and had many memories associated with it. Rambilasji Ghagshyan, Mahavirji Noondwala and Anand Swaroop ji's family owned agricultural lands and fruit orchards (Bagh) in the vicinity of Okara, in Gogera, in Karman Wala, and in Marula (North of Renala Khurd). Gogera used to be District Headquarters prior to Montgomery-Sahiwal during British Rule. Headmasterji grew up in Lahore in college days, but Okara was like rural heart of Lahore. Usman Muhammad Khan was a kid of around 10 yrs during those days and used to take tuitions from Headmasterji. Usman Muhammad Khan, is now based at New Jersey, USA, headmasterji's eldest son- Om prakash Sharma also 80 yrs (now settled in Jaipur), Mahavirji Sharma's eldest son Surendra-settled in Pilani- and many other who visited Okara still have memories about that mill.

Sutluj Cotton Mill's cultural committee would organize different cultural events in the premises. They used to have mushaira and kavi sammelan in Satluj cotton mills' auditorium which was biggest in those days inside the mill compound. A mushaira, conference of poets, was held in the *Sutlej Cotton Mills, Okara* in which several poets from different parts of country including Calcutta were invited.

Many hindi and urdu poets including Iqbal, used to recite their poems and Headmasterji had developed a liking for urdu during those days, he had infact learnt urdu, and even after return from Okara he used to write letters to his grand son Sushil Sharma in urdu, whose copies are still available with them in Jaipur

Headmasterji liked these lines a lot:

Hum Na Honge To Hume Yaad Karegi Duniya...

Apne Jeene Ki Ada Bhi Anokhi Sab Se
Apne Marne Ka Bhi Andaaz Nirala Hoga

Ek Din Bik Jayega, Maati Ke Mol
Jag Mein Reh Jayenge Pyare Tere Bol

Dooje Ke Hothon Ko Dekar Apne Geet
Koi Nishani Chhor, Phir Duniya Se Dol

Relocation to Okara

Rambilas ji moved to Okara. His sister Godavari Devi remembered those as the golden days.

Picture Reference 17: Birla High School, Okara, lahore

Picture Reference 18: Headmasterji as Head of Birla High School, Okara, Lahore(sitting row-5th from left: Headmasterji in black coat)

An account of Appointment of Rambilasji Sharma at Sutluj Cotton Mills, Okara(Lahore district, Punjab, Now in Pakistan)

Mr Rajgarhia who was a management trainee, and working in other Birla mill at Delhi was appointed manager of the mill. But due to initial delay of 3-4 yrs in installation phase at Satluj Cotton Mills, the company suffered losses.

GD Birla questioned Mr.Rajgarhia, the manager at Sutluj Cotton Mills, who resigned. GD Birla called upon Sh. Muralidharji Dalmia to take the additional charge of Sutluj Cotton Mills, as the warehouse incharge. But Sh. Muralidharji was already occupied with other responsibilities and was handling the Birla Mill at Delhi, he did not accept Birla ji's proposal. In discussion with Muralidharji, GD Birla, got the reference of a very familiar name to him- "Mr. Rambilasji". Murlidhar ji told Birlaji that Rambilasji was suitable for this position. GD Birla, without any further discussion, concluded that this could be the right choice. Murlidharji said "He would be available as a trouble shooter there in delhi. and would come to Okarra as and when required". He knew the potential of Rambilas ji very well and has closely observed that. So, he called upon Rambilas ji to take the additional responsibility of Sutluj Cotton mills as warehouse incharge. Rambilas ji accepted this, as his brother in law Mahaveerji was already employed there in the dairy section. This was another recognition bestowed upon Rambilasji, within a year from his promotion to the Principal of School. He got the quarter in the Mill compound.

After the partition in 1947, the factory at Okara was seized by the government of Pakistan. In the year 1963, SIL established Rajasthan Textile Mills (RTM) at Bhawanimandi, District Jhalawar, Rajasthan, to produce cotton yarn. In 1970, it diversified into synthetic blended yarn.

Sutlejcotton was also one of the prominent manufacturers of cotton and cotton blended dyed and melange yarn in the country. The company has two major units producing synthetic and blended yarns and 100% yarns. It manufactures cotton goods including dhotis, drills, saris, bed sheets, towels and twills. It is an integrated player in the textiles industry with a value chain extending from yarn at one end and extending to fabric, garments and home textiles at the other, enabling it to address opportunities in every intervening segment.

The life at Sutluj Cotton Mills, was one of the best periods, of Rambilasji's life. His salary was Rs. 300, which was a big amount. When he went to Surajgarh to celebrate Diwali with his family in 1945, he talked to his parents, to shift his wife and children-Omprakash ji, Satyaprakash ji and Gayatri devi ji, to Okara and hence, moved his family to Okara in November 1945. He had a quarter in the Mill compound. It was well constructed with six bungalows in a row. They had all facilities within the compound. The compound had a swimming pool and all other recreational facilities. Omprakash Ji and Satya Prakash ji were admitted to Birla School, Okara.

Okara had fruit orchards and dry fruit farms. Mahaveer Prasad ji and Rambilas ji had jointly bought few farms and orchards in Okara. Godavari Devi, sister of Rambilasji and Mahaveer Prasad ji's wife, remembers, "We used to have tons of almonds and cashewnuts from our farms. Since, nobody would eat that much, I would grind them and make almond sweets. There would be no dearth of fruits and vegetables. We had a lavish life there."

Cinema hall at Okara.

Rambilas ji shifted his family to Okara in November, 1943. Although, Rambilas ji himself was not a cinema-goer, but he would take his family to a theatre to watch movie. Venus was the only movie theater in Okara. During those days Mobile Movie Theaters were also erected in open grounds, like an Open Air Theater. Those were called talkies, because before the sound was introduced in the movies, there used to be Silent Movies. Later, with the addition of sound, talkies came into being.

Movie ticket in the hall front rows used to be 6 Aana and back seats 12 Aana (3/4th Rupee). Gallery ticket was one Rupee and 4 Aana. Private Booth ticket used to be very expensive, two Rupees and 4 Aana. Movie Theater prices were the same in Okara, Montgomery, Lyalpur, and Lahore etc. Opposite Venus Cinema was Dehli Wala Mithai Shop, who sold excellent quality sweetmeats and desserts.

As remembered by His eldest son Sh. Om Prakash Ji, who was nine years old at that time, "Headmaster ji never enjoyed films, but once in a while, would take us to theatre. I remember watching movie, "Ram Rajya, Bharat Milap, Shakuntala" at Venus, Okara. We were thrilled to watch these movies. He would take us to watch only those movies, which had some values to be imbibed. He would always ask us, after returning from the theatre, as to what lessons we learnt from the movie."

Picture Reference 19: Godawaridevi-rambilasji's Sister and Mahaveer Prasad ji Noondwala, Rambilasji's Brother-in- law

Rambilasji's Focus

Headmasterji had a poor knowledge of cinema. Once he had been for the Interview for the post of teacher, at Delhi. The interviewer asked him- "Who is Ashok Kumar?"

He Replied, "He was a great king and a great warrior- Ashoka-the-Great".

The interviewer, smiled and said, "Don't you know, Ashok Kumar- A film star."

He candidly replied, "No."

Although he was offered the Job, he denied that, because he felt that the questions posed in the interview, reflected the incompatibility in his focus of life and the school administrator's focus.

Rambilasji's reaction to then Modern day Movie

Ram niwas ji Swami, teacher at Chirawa School, left the school and became incharge of Manprakash talkies at Jaipur. He was a good friend and colleague of Headmaster ji. So, Ram Niwas ji would take Rambilas ji's family to watch movie at Manprakash talkies very often. Since, Rambilasji's kids were growing up; they would always like this proposal. Once the movie, "Praya Dhan" was screened and Rambilasji's eldest son, Om Prakash ji, who lived in Jaipur, in those days, talked to Ramniwas ji and planned to watch this movie. Since, Om prakash ji knew that this was a typical entertainment movie, he could not muster courage to ask his father to accompany him and decided to go with others in the family. But unfortunately, Headmasterji enquired Om prakash ji about the movie he was going for. OmPrakash ji replied, "Paraya Dhan." Headmasterji said, "This must be a good movie, about daughters, who leave their parents after they get married. It must be a family movie. I want to come with you." Omprakash ji knew that headmasterji's perception about movie was not correct. But he could not say anything to his father and went for the movie.

After the movie, Ramniwas ji, asked his friend, Rambilas ji, "How was the movie?"

Rambilasji said, "I was mistaken by the title of the movie and mistook it as a family movie. I didn't like the movie. It was a movie around a girl and a boy."

The Strike at Satluj cotton mills Okara and SardarPatel 1945: Strike at Mill and visit of Sarder Vallabh bhai Patel

Picture reference 20: Sarder Patel and GD Birla at Birla guest house- Okara, Lahore

Muhommad Ali Jinnah who was President of Muslim League was to speak to the workers in the Satluj Cotton Mills. In those days the staff of the Birlas at Satluj Cotton Mills were all Marwaris(Hindus from Pilani region of Rajasthan), and the supervisior and the workers were all Punjabi muslims, who were localites.

Jinnahinstigated the workers by addressing, "All the workers at Sutluj cotton mills are Muslims and that is the reason why all of you are being paid lesser wages. You must stand up for higher wages. Birlas are not going to give heed to your demands easily and hence, you must declare strike." Hence the workers went on strike in the mill.

An example of this was the strike at Sutlej Cotton Mill. There were also labour shutdowns at Lyallpur Cotton Mills, the Okara Textile Mills and the Bata boot factory.

Hedmasterji was ware house incharge and workers agitating were putting stern demands in front of management. That was unacceptable. GD Birla was informed by Rambilasji Sharma about the strike and the attitude of the workers. GD spoke to Gandhiji, Nehru and other congressmen to intervene, since Satluj Cotton Mills was the largest mill in whole South East Asia in 1945. As the talks of partiions were already surfacing, no one was interested to go to Okara and pacify the workers; only Sarder Patel dared. Sardar Patel travelled all the way to Okara to break the strike. Sarder Patel was known to be an arch rightist, pro-capitalist, anti-labour, and extremely close to the Birlas. Gandhi and most other leaders (other than the two Nehrus), were also close to Birlas, but all of them, unlike Sardar Patel, maintained their distance from the Birlas. Around 1945, there was a strike in Birla Cotton Mills in Okara, which is now in Pakistan. Infact Sarder Patel threatened them all to withdraw the strike or else would starve for the food and shelters, even the Hindu workers supporting the strike were made clear that they would be jailed along with the Muslim workers.

Headmasterji had arranged the dinner for Sarder Patel. Headmasterji's brother in law-Mahavir Prasad Noondhwala-from Pilani was dairy and canteen incharge there in satluj cotton mills. Rambilasji had specialy ordered, and Sarder Patel asked Rambilasji to prepare for shifting back the families to native since the situation of the communal tension was grappling and partition was almost confirm. Sarder Patel even indicated Rambilasji-"You are so qualified and powerful orator, why don't you join politics." But Rambilasji politiely refused citing reasons of old parents and the sole responsibility of bread-earner for the family. Sarder said, "I will ask GD Birla to take you in some other concern in Hindustan." Rambilasji was quite thankful to Sardar for what sarder had done to save his job here, headmasterji had high regards for SardarPatel. (later in his teaching carreer headmasterji often cited Sardar without turban and Iron man of india – for the bold, strong decision making and strong binding attitude and patriotism of Vallabhbhai Patel.). Patel went back.

Later GD Birla appointed Rambilasji to Hindustan Motors in Calcutta/ Chennai. This was first meeting of Rambilasji with Sardar Patel- the Iron Man of India and the architect of modern India.

The partition talks-Okara-Lahore environment:

http://www.dadinani.com/capture-memories/read-contributions/major-events-pre-1950/155-leave-okara-part-1-by-anand-sarup

Lahore in grip of fear:

"I do not know the date. One evening in early 1947, when our family went up to the roof, we found the sky lighted with a huge fire in the direction of the walled city of Lahore. Next morning, the news that one of the oldest settlement of Hindus (inside the Shah Aalami Gate) had been set on fire was circulating in the city," remeninsces Godavari Devi.

There were no modern communication systems. Very few people had cars or bikes, and there were no local buses. Perhaps less than 0.5 percent of households or offices had telephones. In India at that time, there were no TVs. Even in Lahore, which was a relatively modern city, less than 1 percent of the people had radio sets. The government ran the broadcasting system, and never reported any controversial events.

The news about the fire was published but the Tribune, which was (and is even today in India's Punjab) a highly reputed, secular, independent newspaper, had not reported who had set the area on fire and what had followed thereafter. However, the grapevine was very active those days. Muslim Magistrate, Mr. Cheema, had cordoned off the area and stood and watched the area burn, preventing people from escaping. Many people charred in the fire and the mothers threw their children from the first or second storey tenements, to save them from fire.

This horrifying news came as a shock to the citizens of Lahore, a very old city known for its trade, industry, educational institutions and cultural organisations. The old Lahore city was within a fort with gates that had been given names by the Mughal rulers, especially Akbar's son Jahangir, who liked to spend as much time as possible in Lahore. The old city, including the Shah Aalami area, had a roaring trade in textiles, grains, artefacts, etc.

Lahore was in the grip of fear. Rambilas ji was part of a group of secular individuals who were interested in the prevention of spread of violence. His group had a few Muslims and the others were mainly Hindus, with some who, were agnostics. Those days, Rajinder Singh, then about 21 years old, was staying with one of the Rambilas ji's friend's family. (Those days if you had to go and stay in a hotel in a city where you had friends, it was presumed that either you or your friends were boors, incapable of making real friends.) He was the youngest brother of the freedom-fighting martyr Bhagat Singh.

We asked Rajinder, and two other friends, Suraj Bhan and Mohammed Saleem, to go and check up the rumours, especially whether the stories about Cheema were true.

They came back and confirmed that the Magistrate Cheema had used the police force in his charge to prevent people from escaping from their burning homes. This information filled all of us with great anger. Rajinder Singh felt that what Cheema had done was no different from what Saunders was guilty of. And since Cheema had acted like a state protected terrorist, he had to be taught a lesson in precisely the way Rajinder's brother Bhagat Singh had taught a lesson to the state sponsored terrorists in the late 1920s. If Cheema was killed, others in the government would understand that somehow, they too would be punished for their misdeeds.

They had acquired two hand grenades and planned to go to the Mozang Area, where Cheema had his bungalow. The hand grenades came from an ordnance factory in Baghbanpura, very near Lahore. At that time, such weapons had begun leaking out because the system of governance had collapsed.

Until this time, the two of them had never handled a hand grenade. This did not matter to them - they were impassioned, filled with a sense of bravado and even willing to resort to violence. As they neared Cheema's house, they realized they had to test one of the grenades to discover whether it was live or not. They had no idea that it would make a loud noise when it was detonated. The noise of the detonation alerted the *dhobis* (washermen) washing their clothes on a *nullah* (stream) nearly two hundred yards away. The *dhobis* rushed and overpowered the two adventurers.

Next morning, when there was no news in the papers, we concluded that Rajinder and Shinghara had not succeeded in their mission. "But, we were not concerned about their welfare, and assumed that they would show up in due course. I went to the college as usual. At midday, my father sent a person to contact me at the college. He told me that my father was waiting for me at the residence of Mr. Sardul Singh, a lawyer, who was my father's friend and had been with him in Multan jail in the 1942 Do or Die movement.

When I reached there, we had a brief exchange during which Sardul Singh told me that there were arrest warrants against me, and the police had already searched our home. He gave me a thousand rupees - a huge amount considering that a family of five could live comfortably on provisions costing Rs. 20 a month - and told me to go underground to avoid arrest. His fear was that as a non-Muslim, I would be summarily killed in police custody if I were arrested. When I asked him where I should go, he told me not to tell him or anyone else, because police torture could easily make them reveal my whereabouts.

I think this happened in early April 1947. For the next six months, I wandered all over Punjab. I began with a visit to Khatkar, where Bhagat Singh's family lived. I knew that by convention, the police never entered this village and I would be perfectly safe there," as quoted by Anand Swaroop ji.

Politically, the Congress party dominated Okara. The Hindus and the Muslims had always lived in amity there. One of the Hindu friends of Rambilas ji chose to stay back in Okara as even after 14th August 1947, when Pakistan was formed, there had been no violence between Hindus, Muslims, and Sikhs in Okara region. All the people had reconciled to continuing to live on in Pakistan. This is where they had their livelihood, their old neighbours, their homes and the artefacts they were used to. Until then it had been peaceful in Okara, and it was expected that with time, the dust would settle down, and the old equations between the administration and the different communities and their leaders would be re-established.

In Okara, most of the Hindus had accepted the fact of the formation in Pakistan. Pakistan's flag was hoisted in the crossing in front of Rambilasji's friend's home, with the officers of the local administration doing the honours. Even Hindus saluted the flag without any reservations, and even one of them made a little speech urging everyone to commit to serve Pakistan as a loyal citizen. Everything went well for a few days. The wheels of trade continued to revolve slowly but smoothly in this big *mandi* town.

Then tragedy struck. One day, a train came from India with many Muslim refugees. The town rose to the occasion. The refugees were accommodated under tents in the Company garden and provided with every kind of provisions. Some rich traders threw in some bags of almonds and other dry fruits too as a measure of good will. They also arranged for a doctor to visit the Muslim refugee everyday. There was a belief that all the refugees would be comfortably accommodated in a few weeks, and then the life would be back to normal.

But after about ten days, another train came from India, all splattered with flesh and blood, carrying scores of Muslims killed in cold blood and also many women who had been raped most brutally. This gave rise to great tension between Hindus and Muslims, because the Muslims in Okara could not understand the logic of killing people who were already on their way out of India. Neither the local Hindus nor the local Muslims knew how to respond to this situation. On top of it, Pakistan Radio was broadcasting regularly that what had befallen to this trainload of Muslim was happening also to other Indian Muslims trying to get to Pakistan on foot and by trains.

The Muslims among the local Congress workers, who until then had been guarding the Hindus, knew that this was a situation they would never be able to handle. They threw up their hands and asked the non-Muslims to leave their homes, and, as an interim measure until things settled down, go into the relative safety of the walled *mandi.* The Hindus were greatly perturbed and felt that in the circumstances created by Indian Hindus and Sikhs, whom they cursed in the strongest terms, they had no choice but to follow the advice of their Muslim friends.

Even after the arrival of the second train and after we moved into the *mandi* area, the local Muslims were able to ensure that we could still leave the walled *mandi* to visit our homes at least during the daytime.

Communal tensions in Okara

There was a communal tension between Hindus, Sikhs and the Muslims all over India. The local Hindu population had come to believe that their religious identities were in danger. This fear arose largely because the Muslim invaders were better organised and were generally able to defeat the Hindus.

Godavari devi recalled, "While Okara town was relatively peaceful, the people in the countryside around it were determined to drive the non-Muslims out. They saw this as the only way of making a living space for the Muslim refugees. Every night, the villagers around the town congregated and shouted *Allah-o-Akbar* to the strident beating of drums. This created a sense of panic and reinforced the belief that non-Muslims could not survive in this area. Thus, we were left with no choice but to go to India.

There were killing, looting and raping all around. Our names were enough to identify us as Hindus. We knew that it would foolish to hope that such people would either give us the time to explain or they would understand that in spite of our Hindu sounding names, we were agnostics, not Hindus. In any case, to them anyone who was not a Muslim had no place in Pakistan and deserved to die."

When people especially women folk used to leave for India, they would carry cyanide, so that they could escape rape by committing suicide!

Sending Family back to Surajgarh-1946

Picture Reference 21: Caravans moving towards India, after announcement of India- Pakistan partition- Year 1946-47

In year 1946, the rumours were doing rounds about the partition of India and Pakistan. People conjectured that Okara, Lahore would be part of the newly carved out Pakistan. When, Rambilasji also heard of this, he discussed this with Mahaveer ji and both of them decided to send back their families to Surajgarh and Pilani respectively. Since, the atmosphere of partition was aggravating, there were lot of incidences of violence and terror. So, Rambilasji advised Mahaveer ji to accompany both the families back to their native, as it was not safe to send the ladies alone with the kids. So, families of Rambilas ji and Mahaveerji, along with Mahaveerji, left for Surajgarh. Abdul Majid who was one of the close friends of Rambilasji at Lahore had become a rabid Muslim Leaguer because he believed that Hindus and Muslims could not live peacefully together.

Nonetheless, at a personal level, he was a loyal and affectionate friend. So later, he became instrumental in facilitating my family and my brother in law's family to reach India in relative safety. Even after they left Pakistan, he saved some of their valuables and delivered them to my family, at the Wagah Border.

In the words of Godavari Devi, wife of late. Mahaveerji, "We boarded the train with the doctor of our acquaintance. When we boarded the train, suddenly, we heard the shot from the gun. We were terrified. We were not sure that we would reach our destination safely." They reached Meerut and then Gurgaon and later reached to their destination. In Gurgaon they receieved a warm welcome from the arrangement made by Birlas for the migrants of partitions including camps, food, medicine, rest, doctors and financial aid.

Chapter 9

Return from Okara and joining new job after independence in free India

Points to be covered

- **Return of Rambilasji**
- **Job at Hindustan Motors**
- **Meeting with Ramkrishna Dalmiya**
- **Wedding of Bhagwati Devi**
- **Rambilasji's Bangle business**

Chapter 9

Return from Okara and joining new job

Return of Rambilas ji

Rambilas ji left for Surajgarh after partition. He had to confront lot of difficulties. There was massacre and blood all around. Infact, his family members had no hope of his return. He had to disguise himself to look like a Pathan, to save himself from the fanatics. It took him eight months to reach Surajgarh from Okara. Finally family reunited.

Picture Reference 22: Rare Family picture - Year 1948-49

Rambilas ji's job at HINDUSTAN MOTORS LTD

Hindustan motors ltd. Automobiles Manufacturing company and flagship company of the C.K.Birla was established just before Indian independence in 1942, commencing operations in a small assembly plants in part OKHA near Gujarat. The manufacturingfacilities later moved to Uttar Pradesh, West Bengal in 1948, where it began theproduction of the ambassador model.

Rambilas ji came back to Surajgarh, after partition. GD Birla, called him and asked him to join Hindustan motors at Calcutta in 1948.Rambilasji, joined at Hindustan Motors. An American engineer had been called to install the machine imported from America. He would use abusive language. Rambilas ji could understand that, as he had good command over English. So, he asked the authorities to remove this engineer. He was told that they would not keep the engineer for the long time, but since, nobody knew the working of the machinery, it was not wise to expel him. But if Rambilas ji learnt the working from him and develop him, then they would send the engineer back to America.

Meeting with Ramkrishna Dalmia

Picture Reference 23: Headmasterji, RamKrishna Dalmia &GD Birla

When Rambilas ji was working at Hindustan Motors, Birla ji requested him to extend the hospitality to the American engineer who worked at the company. He asked him to take the engineer to the Marwadi Rowing club at Dhakuriya Lake in South Calcutta. In the club the engineer would be busy in drinks (whiskey, beer) but Rambilasji never had drinks, so he would spend his time in the club, playing chess. In the same club, Ramkrishna Dalmia and Jai Dayal Dalmia also used to come and play chess.

Picture Reference 24: Marwari Rowing Club, Howrah

Rambilas ji and Dalmia's developed a strong bonding over chess. They were impressed with Rambilas ji's game. One such day, they were candidly discussing about their personal life that Dalmia ji got to know that Rambilas ji worked at Birlas and hailed from Surajgarh from where RamKrishna Dalmiaji's wife, Durga Devi also hailed, because of which Dalmiaji had a special rapport with Rambilas ji. (Later on Dalmia ji started Durga Devi Dalmia Ayurvedic Aushadhalaya at Surajgarh. It was with the reference of Rambilas ji that Vaidya Madan lalji Pushkarna, who had come from Lahore, Pakistan with Rambilas ji, got the appointment as Vaidya. He served the Aushadhalaya till his death. His Son Arun Pushkarna, still works with the same aushadhalaya.). Dalmia ji enquired Rambilas ji about his salary at Hindustan motors and then offered him double the salary that he was fetching at that time and proposed Headmaster ji to join his company-Meenakshi Chemicals at Kurnool, AndhraPradesh, which was Dalmiaji's firm. Rambilas ji joined there as warehouse Incharge. He even called his elder brother Srinivas ji to Kurnool and offered him to do a business venture – selling the scrap metal tins of chemicals generated from Meenakshi chemicals.

Wedding of Bhagwati Devi organised by Rambilasji

In year 1949, both Srinivasji and Rambilasji, came to Surajgarh on the occasion of the wedding of Bhagwati devi, Srinivasji's eldest daughter. Bhagwati devi got married to Bhedas of Chirawa. The marriage was the grand affair in history of Ghagshyans –credited to Rambilasji. Rambilas ji spent lavishly on the wedding. It was the first wedding of that generation and Rambilas ji did not want to leave any gap in the arrangements.

Some of the employees of Meenakshi Chemicals also attended the wedding. They were astonished to witness the grandeur of the wedding. On the return to Kurnool, they complaint about the grandeur of wedding to the management. They doubted that since Rambilas ji was helping Srinivas ji in scrap business, they might be involved in making money by wrong means. Since, Ramkrishna Dalmia knew Rambilas ji very closely, he defied such complaints but when Rambilas ji got to know about such complaint and his self- respect got hurt and he decided not to return to Kurnool. Although Dalmia ji called him again to join the duty and told him that he had already taken action against those who complaint against Rambilas ji, hence there was no discordance, but Rambilas ji did not change his decision.

Ram bilas ji's bangles business

Rambilasji went to Calcutta but Rambilas ji did not send money order for six months, which otherwise he regularly sent from wherever he worked earlier. Gajnanada ji was worried and decided to go to Calcutta to look into the matter. After reaching Calcutta, Rambilasji discussed with him about his employement. He had ventured in the Bangle industry, in partnership with Agarwal (Halwai) from Pilani. They were into the manufacturing of Bangles. But looking into the account books, gave the right picture to Gajanada ji and he could make out that the business was into losses. Rambilas ji had invested all his money into this venture but was realized by Gajanand ji that his partner cheated him, since Rambilas ji was a non-commercial business man. Gajanand ji, settled the accounts and ordered Rambilas ji to return to Surajgarh with Gajanand ji.

Picture Reference 25: Surajgarh first electionrally, where the then ruler Raja Raghubir singh, addressing a rally- most of the prominent personalities of Surajgarh are seen in the picture including Headmasterji.

PART IV

BACK TO SURAJGARH

Chapter 10

PB High School Days 1950-1972

Points covered

- **Rambilasji's relocation to Surajgarh & Gilluram Bharatiya**
- **Command over English**
- **Motivating and Mentoring students**
- **Rambilasji's Discipline**
- **Chattar Singh ji**
- **Hemdutt Ji Mathur**

Chapter 10

PB High School Days 1950-1972

Photo reference 26: PB high School, Surajgarh Ram Bilas ji & Gilluram Bahratiya- Rambilasji's relocation to Surajgarh

Gilluramji Bharatiya was class mate of Rambilasji from Chirawa high school days.

Gilluram Bharatiya was secretary of PB High School from 1941 to 1963. Headmasterji and gilluram bharathia were classmates and also close friends from school days. When headmasterji's father Shri Gajanandji passed away in 1950, Gilluramji Bharatiya visited headmasterji's home. Gilluramji used to call headmasterji's mother as "Maa". Maa told Gilluramji "gilluram ib mhain log ekla ho ga hain, ib Rambilas nain urre hi school main rakhano hain.". Gilluram ji replied, "Maa Rambilasji bahut zyada padheda hain, aur yo Birla ke Okara mill main unchi post par hain. Inki pagar bhi jyada hain, mhain itna jyada pisa koni de sakan." Maa insisted," Nahin ib yo urre hiin rahavego"

Since Rambilas ji had lot of respect for his mother, he accepted his mother's decision to relocate to Surajgarh and Gilluram Bharatiya was honoured to have a highly qualified teacher at PB high School. Rampratapji was head masterji of PB High School in those days.

Rambilasji was quite high qualified, and had better knowledge of English. In spite of being headmaster, Rampratapji had high regards in the school and he use to consult Rambilasji in important matters of school.

This is how Rambilasji joined PB High school., which was then by the efforts of Rambilasji Sharma got upgraded and permitted to become-PB high school. The photograph below indicates the Function of PB high school, indicates the presence of His highness – King Raghubir Singhji, Mr. Menon –Government of India representative and Fatehchandji from PB high school.

Picture Reference 27: PB high School foundation day, Surajgarh- in the photo are seen From L-to-R: lower row: Raghubir singh (In goggles), Mr.Menon, Fatehchandji, From R to L(upper row): Chottelalji Vaidya, Gilluram Bharatia, Rambilasji Sharma, Amarsinghji Postmasterji and others.

Rambilasji Headmasterji and Shri Krishna Parishad, prabhat library

Picture Reference 28: Sri Krishna Parishad, Surajgarh

Shree Krishna Parishad: Prabhat libray was the vision of Heamasterji Shri. Rambilasji Sharma. In 1931-32 he was the first graduate of the jhunjunu district, and in 1936 became the first post graduate from Lahore University in Surajgarh-Jhunjhunu district. The financial committee was of his students.

The committe had Gaurishanker Kayan, Murlidhar Dalmia, Tulsiram Shah, Visvanath Kanodia and Jugal Kishor Barasiya-who was headmasterji's favorite student.

The beauty of headmasterji's nature -he would never get indulged/ interfere into the routine/day to day and financial matters of the organisation. This shows his sincerity, honesty, straight forwardness and selflessness. He would not take any post of power, would quietly guide and let the others enjoy power and ego.

Shri Krishna Parishad which is one of the oldest organisations working for social and cultural activities at Surajgarh, was founded in 1931, and actively had a reading centre after 1939. After Rambilasji Sharma Post Graduated from Lahore University and came back to Surajgarh, he wanted a reading centre and a centre for cultural association for the learned people in Surajgarh, and thus came the first library. The daily newspapers like Punjab Kesari used to be regular in library.

Headmasterji Rambilasji Sharma was one of founder member supporting it with other the Prabhat Pustakalaya is one of the library serving Surajgarh.

Headmasterji never indulged in any politics and name game. infact immediately after coming back from Okara, Lahore, Punjab(now in Pakistan), in 1948, Choumal offered the president post for Rambilasji, which Headmasterji declined saying, please don't indulge me in any political post, and recommended name of his friend Shri Madanlal Pushkarna whom hedmasterji has brought with himself from Lahore, Punjab after partition, and hence is still called sharnarthi vaidhhyaji. Headmasterji guided the work of the parishad from outside. His close friends were head of parishad from 1936-till 1975.

It was on request of his good friends like Babulalji Halwai, Madanlalji Pushkarna, Ramniranjan Choumal, Babulalji Choudhary, Gilluram Bharatia and others he became president of Shri Krishna parishad, Surajgarh in 1964-65 and celebrated silver jublee of the organisation in 1968, people still remember the activities and participation, where Headmasterji call his friend from chirawa school days, Shri. Hajarilalji Sharma- MLA as chief guest. The formal event was anchored by Headmasterji/s student and local politician Mahavirprasad Sharma-chairman.

The crux is headmsterji always guided the path of the people and for the betterment of social life of people of Surajgarh, in terms of education, social cause, activities, and cultural cause.

Picture Reference 29: After flag hosting on 15th august at Sri Krishna Parishad, Surajgarh

Rambilas ji's command over English

Rambilasji was the English teacher in those times. Till 1955, Sh.Ram Pratap ji was a Principal. Ram Bilas ji was better qualified than Ram Pratapji. Hence, Rampratap ji always hold him in high esteem, as he knew the potential of Rambilasji. He knew that Rambilas ji had higher qualifications than him and also had good exposure.

As has been narrated by Shri Matadin ji Khandelwala, who was student of Class X in 1956 at PB High School, "Rambilas ji had a very distinctive courage and quality of being generous. He never gave importance to money. He had good command over English. When he would teach Prose on Shakespere, he would handle the difficult words and their meanings separately."

Motivating and mentoring the students- Omkar Mal Agarwal (Surajgarh Mandi)

Shri Omkar Agarwal of Surajgarh Mandi, passed class X in 1966, he narrated, "I was shy and introvert. Headmasterji wanted me to participate in debate competition. I went to Headmasterji and confessed that I did not know what to speak, how to speak and would not be able to withstand the gathering. I won't be able to utter a single word. I am not confident. Listening to this, headmasterji did not give up rather gave personal coaching to me and wrote a debate script for me and made sure that I practice the debate in front of mirror. His motivation gave me courage and I stood second in the competition. It was indeed a great pleasure to receive the certificate from the hands of Shri Haribhau Upadhyay, then Education Minister of Rajasthan, who has come to host flag on 15 th august in 1966. This boosted my confidence and changed me for the life time. I still remember what he said about Headmasterji in his speech that the young generation was fortunate enough to have Rambilas ji as their guide, teacher and philosopher. It was sure that wherever these students would go they would shine and excel in whatever they do. It was not because of a system but because of an incarnation of God and true educationalist- Rambilasji. I pay my gratitude to Rambilas ji for the successful life as a business man."

Ram bilas ji and caning 1966

In 1966, a maths teacher joined PB High School, who did his PTC from North India. He wrote a question on the board: If a man does "X" work in one day, how much time would he take to finish the work? Headmaster ji taught maths to his youngest son SunitiKumar ji and would make him do all sums at home before they were done in the class.

The maths teacher wrote wrong question on the board. As Suniti Kumar ji was prepared, he knew the question was wrong. He stood up and pointed out to the teacher that the question was wrong. The teacher felt it insulting and he caught Suniti ji by his hair and took him to Headmasterji's office. He complaint, "Principal Saab, your son behaves arrogantly in front of other students in the class. He is saying that the question I have written on board is wrong. This taints the image of a teacher"

Headmasterji immediately took out the cane and caned him twice and warned him not to repeat such behaviour and sent him back to the class. This is how he exhibited fair and disciplined behaviour at school.

Afte Sunitikumar ji left, headmaster ji asked the teacher to write the question on the board. The teacher wrote the question, which was actually wrong. Headmaster ji told the teacher not to commit mistakes in the class.

Picture reference 30: Head masterji taking guard of honour of NCC wing on 26th January 1960.In the picture are seen Madanlal Pushkarna Vaidyaji, Mahavirprasad Sharma-chairman and others.

Year 1969
Chatar Singh Kothari (Sultanpur)

Chatar Singh ji was from the affluent Jat family of Raghunathpura. His father and Uncle worked with Birlas. Once his father and Uncle asked him to talk to Headmaster ji, as they wanted to meet him. They sent for Headmasterji. Headmaster ji agreed to come but told Chatar Singh ji, "It would take me half an hour as I leave home after the breakfast only. If you prefer, you can also join me for breakfast."

Chatar Singh returned and told this to his father and Uncle. They were impressed and told Chatar Singh to always remember not to leave home empty stomach.

Headmaster ji taught him till standard tenth. During that time, he stayed with Headmaster ji and he was given all facilities- food, lodging etc. free of cost. He was not the only student, who studied and stayed for free, but there were many more.

When Chatar Singh performed well in tenth exams, his father came to meet Headmasterji and touched his feet for all that support, and that too without any cost for so many years. His father offered to sow a five bigha land for Headmasterji and proposed that headmasterji would get the yield of that 5 bigha throughout his life. But Headmasterji refused to take this favour.

Not only this, but headmasterji arranged for his further studies at Agrawala College, Jaipur. He asked his eldest son Shri OmPrakash ji to help Chatar singhji for at least six months and provide him the lodging and food.

Headmasterji gave affection of Parents and teacher. Although he was an individual but helped the society as the Institution.

Year 1951-62- The golden era of Indian Football,

During this time all school started promoting their student to participate in the football game, developed school teams, and participated in interstate tournaments. PB high school was on a high in football, and Rambilasji himself promoted and played football, he even encouraged his staff teachers to play and learn to development personality if the individual- like team spirit, focus, goal, strategy, action.

Sultan Singh- Athletics- 1965-66 state champion.

NCC was given inter service image in 1952 and Pandit Jawahar Lal Nehru recommended it to be part a part of NCC syllabus and development of NCC in major places in India.

Headmasterji took active interest in the development of NCC in Surajgarh, Chirawa, Pilani and Jhunjhunu. He encouraged students to join NCC. He would himself monitor and would be part of these activities.

After Indo-China war in 1962, Jawahar Lal Nehru made NCC compulsory. Infact Surajgarh, Chirawa, Pilani in Jhunjhunu District had

NCC since 1952, ten years before it was made compulsory in 1962, as a result of which there were good number of soldiers who fought in Indo China war from this region.

Rambilas ji was a patriot and as a teacher, the selfless desire to serve the nation was already there being incharge of NCC at Surajgarh. He would himself be a part of group in social service camp, Routine PT camps, NCC parades. Infact headmasterji was honoured to take salute of parade at PB High school.

Picture Reference 31: PB High School Football Team, as a winner of BL Maheshwari Football Trophy, Baggar, With Headmaster ji in the centre.

He organized Republic day camp, Combined Annual Training camps, National Integrated camps and All india Summer training camps. He would himself, accompany his cadets to the other parts of country to attend the camps. As those were the days, when the commutation to the other parts of India was not smooth and convenient, Parents would be reluctant to allow their wards to attend such camps in other states. Headmasterji knew this and hence, to convince the Parents he would accompany the cadets, ensuring their complete safety to their parents. Even Parents would be rest assured that their children were in the right hands. Once he took the cadets to the camp in Hyderabad in 1963, where he made arrangements with the help of his relative, Col. KL Sharma, who was posted in the Hyderabad cantonment during those days. In those days, the commutation from Rajasthan to Hyderabad was pain and used to take 4 Days to reach Hyderabad. So, It was challenge for him to not only persuade the cadets but also their parents, as they were unsecured about the long distance travel. But to everybody's surprise he could convince the parents and assured them the well- being of their wards and accompanied them to Hyderabad. Not only that he arranged for free Lodging and Boarding of Surajgarh Group.

Picture Reference 32: Headmasterji with NCC cadets

He would encourage students to utilize their summer vacation by taking part in NCC camps and serve the nation. He contributed a lot in developing and increasing strength of NCC Cadets in Jhunjhunu district. This had been source of inspiration for the natives of this district and they joined armed forces and hence, Headmasterji was instrumental in bringing proud to Jhunjhunu district of offering highest number of armed personnel.

Picture Reference 33: Mass Drill Exercise carried out at PB High School during the Headmasterji's tenure

Picture Reference 34: Seth Fateh Chand ji Jhunjhunwalia, the Founder trustee of PB High School addressing the students on Foundation day.

Picture Reference 35: Purshottam Lal Jhunjhunuwala, Managing Trustee of PB High School addressing students- Year 1968

Photo reference no. 36: PB High School Staff -1962-63

Photo reference no 37: Then Education Minister of Rajasthan Sh. Haribhau Upadhyay at PB High School Foundation Day

Photo Reference No. 38: First Chamber of Commerce members' visit to Surajgarh

Photo reference no. 39: Headmasterji addressing Shree Krishna Parishad as President

Photo Reference 40:Headmasterji with Guru Hanuman

Chapter 11

Life after PB High School

Points covered

- **Rambilasji at Farah**
- **Rambilasji at RaghunathPura**
- **Rambilasji at Ishwarpura**
- **Shree Krishna Parishad**
- **Rambilasji's book Donated**

Chapter 11

Life after PB High School

Rambilas ji at Farah

Rambilas ji joined Seth Premsukhdas college at Farh as Director in 1972. After that from 1974 to 1975 he worked at Agrawala High School, Vallabhgarh as DIrector. Narendra Singh Gupta was the trustee of the school and he and his family respected Headmasterji as fatherly figure. Headmaster ji had instrumental role in development of the school. He hired well educated teachers and even started English medium education. But then due to ailing health, he returned to Surajgarh.

RamBilas ji and Raghunath Pura Year 1965-69

SultanRam Kothari was Rambilas ji's friend, who stayed in Raghunathpura. He used to visit Raghunathpura very often to meet him. There was nobody in the whole village who was as learned as Headmasterji. So whenever he visited Raghunathpura, he would sit on the cot and all other sat down. Those days Jats were not very educated. Headmaster ji preached them, "If you want to prosper, educate your children. Give equal status to girls and educate them. To keep the light of kuldeepak intact, a girl, a mother and a woman should be educated. If a girl is educated she would teducate his kids also."

Thus, Headmaster ji tried to revolutionize the jat community and farmers to educate. He was the proponent of education in this region.

School at Ishwarpura

Immediately after retiring from PB High School in 1971, Rambilas ji joined Seth Ishwardas Tekriwal madhyamik vidyalaya at Ishwarpura, Jhunjhunu district. Ishwarpura village was around 20 miles from Jhunjhunu. It was not possible to commute everyday between Jhunjhun u and Ishwarpura, at the age of 58 years. Moreover the water of the wells at Ishwarpura had hard and salty water. Headmasterji stayed at Ishwardasji's Dharamshaala at Ishwarpura only. Since, the proper water and food was not available in Ishwarpura, the in-laws of Rambilasji's son Sh Savita Prakash ji, used to send food and water every day for Rambilas ji through an employee of the same school, who commuted every day from Jhunjhunu to Ishwarpura. Headmaster ji appointed Sh. Rajendra Sharma in the same school, who worked there for six months. Later Rajendra ji got the opportunity as a clerk in the government school, but the requirement of the job was two years work experience. Rajendra ji reminisces, "When I got this offer, I was into fix. Although I have worked for more than two years but had no experience certificate, as I worked on the daily basis. Ishwarpura job was my first job as the full time employee which was only for six months. I was not sure and discussed this matter with headmaster ji. Knowing my earlier work experience, he had been kind enough to give me the certificate of two years of work experience. This changed my life and I lead my life comfortably. I retired in the year 2012, and because of his support, I am a pensioner and am secured. I owe this to Headmasterji."

Role of Rambilas Sharma in Shree Krishna Parishad, Surajgarh

Shree Krishna Parishad: Prabhat libray was the vision of Heamasterji Shri. Rambilasji Sharma. In 1931-32 he was the first graduate of the Jhunjunu district, and in 1936 became the first post graduate from Lahore University in Surajgarh-Jhunjhunu district. The financial committee was of his students.

The committe had Gaurishanker Kayan, Murlidhar Dalmia, Tulsiram Shah, Visvanath Kanodia and Jugal Kishor Barasiya-who was headmasterji's favorite student.

The beauty of headmasterji's nature -he would never get indulged/ interfere into the routine/day to day and financial matters of the organisation.

This shows his sincerity, honesty, straight forwardness and selflessness. He would not take any post of power, would quietly guide and let the others enjoy power and ego.

Shri Krishna Parishad which is one of the oldest organisations working for social and cultural activities at Surajgarh, was founded in 1931, and actively had a reading centre after 1939. After Rambilasji Sharma Post Graduated from Lahore University and came back to Surajgarh, he wanted a reading centre and a centre for cultural association for the learned people in Surajgarh, and thus came the first library. The daily newspapers like Punjab Kesari used to be regular in library.

Headmasterji Rambilasji Sharma was one of founder member supporting it with other the Prabhat Pustakalaya is one of the library serving Surajgarh.

Headmasterji never indulged in any politics and name game. infact immediately after coming back from Okara, Lahore, Punjab(now in pakistan), in 1948, Choumal offered the president post for Rambilasji, which Headmasterji declined saying, please don't indulge me in any political post, and recommended name of his friend Shri Madanlal Pushkarna whom hedmasterji has brought with himself from Lahore, Punjab after partition, and hence is still called sharnarthi vaidhhyaji. Headmasterji guided the work of the parishad from outside. His close friends were head of parishad from 1936-till 1975.

It was on request of his good friends like babulalji halwai, madanlalji pushkarna, ramniranjan choumal, babulalji choudhary, gilluram bharatia and others he became president of Shri Krishna parishad, Surajgarhin 1964-65 and celebrated silver jublee of the organisation in 1968, people still remember the activities and participation, where Headmasterji call his friend from chirawa school days, Shri. Hajarilalji Sharma- MLA as chief guest. The formal event was anchored by Headmasterji/s student and local politician Mahavirprasad Sharma-chairman.

The crux is headmsterji always guided the path of the people and for the betterment of social life of people of Surajgarh, in terms of education, social cause, activities, and cultural cause.

Books of Rambilas ji donated-1978

Head Masterji was also Ayurvedachary. This Was conveyed to us by Shri Savitaprakash Sharma, son of Late Shri Rambilasji. After His

Death, All His Classic Collection Of Books On Ayurveda Was Donated To Madanlalji Baidji.

All His Collection on English Literature and English Dictionaries were Donated To Tripathiji.

PART V

MEMORIES OF RAMBILAS JI THROUGH THE EYES OF HIS PEERS, FRIENDS AND STUDENTS

Chapter 12

Memories

Points covered

- **Umashanker Sharma**
- **Madan Lal Pushkarna**
- **Omprakashji Verma**
- **Chattar Singh Kothari**
- **Sisramji Ola**
- **Jugal Kishore Barasiya**
- **Muralidhar Badarika**
- **Omkar mal Agarwal**
- **Suresh Kumar Saini**
- **Hemdutt ji Mathur**
- **Umashanker Poliwala**
- **Jugal Kishore Chawala**

Chapter 12

Memories

Uma Shanker Sharma's memories of Rambilasji

Shri. Umashankar Sharma(Poliwala, Surajgarh) commemorated, "Head masterji has such a reputation in Surajgarh, When after school hours he would start from PB High school to his home, at every step one or the other would do namaskar/charan sparsh through out in bazar and upto his home. such a huge respect and luv he receieved through out his life."

Madan Lal Pushkarna and Headmaster ji's friendship

Picture Reference 41: Madan Lal Pushkarna and Headmaster ji

In 1970, ML Pushkarna, took his son Arun Pushkarna, for admission to PB High School. Sh. Rambilas ji was the Principal of PB High School. Headmasterji was very down to earth. When Madan Lal ji reached school, he asked peon to seek appointment of Rambilas ji. As the peon informed Rambilas ji about Madan Lal ji's request, Headmaster ji stood up and went out to receive him and said, "Bhai Saab, Aapne kyun taklif ki, Mujhe bula liya hota."

Madan lal ji Pointed towards Arun and said, "He is my son. I have come here for his admission to Class VI."

Arun Puskarna recalls, "Hearing this, in a fraction of second, headmaster ji said that you are admitted to school in standard VI A. This made me feel that headmaster ji was humble and down to earth. He had respect for his relations. Besides that the promptness with which he gave me admission along with the Division, made me realize that he was through with his work".

Headmasterji had appointed Vaidhya Madan lal ji, for the regular health check up of the students. In lieu of which he was paid Rs. 300, which would help him financially.

Pitra Paksh Ekadashi and Rambilas ji's love for his forefathers

The male progeny of Rambilas ji's clan expired on Ekadashi and hence, shradha tarpan of all males was done on Ekadashi during the Pitra Paksh.

On Shradh paksh Ekadashi, he would feed 100-150 people with Kheer-Puri, to satiate his ancestors.

Madan lal ji Pushkarna remembers and narrates, "On this day, Rambilas ji would instruct his family to prepare kheer of 50 kg Milk, Pudi, jalebi and Sabzi. He would invite all his relatives and friends for the feast. He would personally come to me, to invite me for the lunch and would insist that, if I would not come, he would not take lunch. This was the affection he had."

Rambilasji and Om Prakash ji Verma

Prakashwati Om Prakash Verma, wife of Late Shri Om Prakash ji Verma- a Science teacher, travelling through the memory lane says, "My husband joined PB Highschool as a Science teacher in 1959. We were newly wedded. Since, we did not know anybody, headmasterji helped us settle down in Surajgarh. He was our Guardian. He helped us to get the Quarter to stay in.

Not as the Principal of the school, but otherwise also all teachers, addressed him as "Guru ji". We used to regard him as an elder brother and a fatherly figure.

Upon birth of both my son, the name – "Vedprakash Verma" was suggested by Rambilasji Headmasterji. Both my sons are now settled in their profession and life having got married and having kids. It is his blessings in the form of the names, we remember guruji as and when we called our son by names.

The environment of the school was good. Guruji was an idealistic. He was good teacher, good Headmaster, a good human being, a good friend, a good social worker and also a good cultural sports guide.

He would make sure that we had no problems. He would visit our quarter after the school time, to check if we had any problem.

There used to be cultural events in the school and everybody participated in that- teachers, their family and students. I still remember the drama which were staged- Raja Harish Chandra, Daanveer karna, Shravan Kumar, Karma Phal, Snehabandhan, Suprabhat, Satyavaan Savitri, Shakuntala, Bhakt Narsimehta, Mira Bai, Shri Krishna- Sudama. He was an Educational Leader. He would take personal care of his teaching as well as non- teaching staff. He considered all as his family. He fulfilled his duty not only as Principal but also as father, Guru and an elder.

Guru ji christened both my sons- Ved Prakash Verma and Girish Kumar Verma. Today they are leading happy and successful life and still remember Guruji. We came from Uttar Pradesh, but stayed back for ever in Surajgarh, only because of Headmasterji.

Unke Jaisa Vyaktitva, Hazaroon Saal mein ek Baar avatarit hota hai. Mera Unko Saadar Pranam, Meri Shraddhanjali"

This reiterates Rambilas ji's wonderful personality and his helping nature.

Omkar Mal Agarwal

Shri Omkar Agarwal of Surajgarh Mandi, passed class X in 1966, he narrated, "I was shy and introvert. Headmasterji wanted me to participate in debate competition. I went to Headmasterji and confessed that I did not know what to speak, how to speak and would not be able to withstand the gathering. I won't be able to utter a single word. I am not confident. Listening to this, headmasterji did not give up rather gave personal coaching to me and wrote a debate script for me and made sure that I practice the debate in front of mirror. His motivation gave me courage and I stood second in the competition. It was indeed a great pleasure to receive the certificate from the hands of Shri Haribhau Upadhyay, then Education Minister of Rajasthan, who has come to host flag on 15th august in 1966. This boosted my confidence and changed me for the life time. I still remember what he said about Headmasterji in his speech that the young generation was fortunate enough to have Rambilas ji as their guide, teacher and philosopher. It was sure that wherever these students would go they would shine and excel in whatever they do. It was not because of a system but because of an incarnation of God and true educationalist- Rambilasji. I pay my gratitude to Rambilas ji for the successful life as a business man."

Rambilasji's Discipline- Shri Suresh Saini

One of the old student of PB high school Shri Suresh saini ji now in Mount Abu, Rajasthan reminisces "I have heard that Headmasterji was very punctual of time and strict Disciplinarian.

He always encouraged "Guru-Shisya Relationship." As a GURU he was very keen to correct spelling and English pronunciation which was rarely available those days. As an administrator he was very very strict even teachers were reprimanded and warned, if they made mistake. He had

High moral with sound character and was charming personality. I have lots of regards for him.

Bhagwan ki banayi ek Anupam bhent they vo. Is Duniya ko aur khoobsurat banane ke liye."

Hemduttji Mathur and Rambilas ji

Hemdutt ji Mathur was teacher with Headmasterji at Dalmia School in Chirawa. He was close friend of Headmasterji. Hemdutt ji used to work as government servant in Jaipur. His Son Prahlad Duttji Mathur is still known to Shri. Savita Prakash ji Sharma, Headmasterji's son. Headmasterji helped the younger brother of Hemduttji, when he was jobless. He hired him in PB High School and then confirmed him on Payroll at the pay scale of Rs. 300 per month. He was grateful to Headmasterji, as this was much needed help in their financially weak condition. Two years later, both the brothers got the government job and moved to Jaipur. Hemdutt ji got the job in the Education Research Department in Government of Rajasthan. He got an opportunity to be with Headmasterji, when he was deputed for the educational research in the Shekhawati region. The research findings were published in the form of book, which had a chapter on the services of Rambilas ji as the Educationist of Rural Rajasthan.

Uma Shanker Poliwala "Rambilas ji: Revered Person of Surajgarh"

Uma Shanker Poliwala, remembers headmaster ji as most revered person of Surajgarh. He narrated, "Headmaster ji was such a respectful person that whenever he left from PB High school to go home, at least 250-300 people would bow and touch his feet, in the belt of 500 meters, before he reached home. He would not stop anywhere in the market and would head towards his home".

No other person before or after him could command so much of respect from the people of Surajgarh. This is the best example of Rural and Charismatic Leadership.

Sisramji Ola And Rambilas ji

Shri. Sisramji Ola, then Union Minister for HRD, attended the wedding of Headmasterji's grandson, Sandeep Sharma, on 15th February 2002. On this occasion, remembering Rambilas ji, he said, "Headmasterji was gem of a person. I remember, during my school days, We had final exams at PB high school. We used to study at Headmasterji's house. It was very difficult to commute twice from Arrawata to Surajgarh. So to facilitate this, we used to stay at Headmasterji's house. So headmasterji used to give free coaching and guidance at home, and I used to live there for complete duration of examination, free lodging, free food, and free preparation for exams. It is because of his ashirwaad, that today I am able to serve the people of nation.".

Jugal Kishore Barasia

Sandeep Sharma, grandson of Rambilas ji,(The Author) had been to Mumbai in 1996-97, and happened to meet Jugal Kishoreji Barasiya, who was the student of Rambilasji Headmasterji. He was thrilled to meet him. Jugal Kishore ji Barasiya said, "Masterji, ki main bahot ijjat karron, main satvi(7) class tak hi padiyo hun, masterji se hi padhyo, meri jindgi main, itno badiya aadmi nain dekhyo. -mahare se kadheyi kuch bhi nahin liyo, main aaj jo bhi kuch hoon, un ki vajah se hoon. our bhi bohut baar kahto- aapne gaon main college koni. en liya ek college banai."

Jugal Kishore ji did not study much but whatever he studied, was from Rambilasji. He attributes all his success to him. Headmasterji never took any favors from anybody and hence when once he mentioned that Surajgarh need college, Barasiya ji took the opportunity to fulfil his Guru's dream. The first degree college of Surajgarh came into existence after that- Barasiya Degree College, Surajgarh.

Murliadhar Badrika:

Murlidhar Badriaka was among the favourite student of Headmasterji. Murlidharji studied higher schooling under Rambilasji and was appointed in the library by Headmasterji since his financial conditions was not good. he joined in the library and Headmasterji helped him in his further studies first graduation and then post graduation. Then he was promoted to a teacher. when asked about Headmasterji Murlidharji said "Rambilasji Headmasterji my guruji, to devta aadmi tha(Headmasterji was a divine figure.)

Such a great person Rambilasji was. He helped the youth to educate, get job and be a honourable citizen of the society.

Dungermal Gupta and Saligram Gupta

As per the talks I had with Sevaramji Gupta (BJP Leader- Surajgarh and Dungermal gupta's Son) Head masterji had very good relation with Dungermal Gupta, who was student Of Rambilassharma during the initial phase of Teaching at PB high School, and later became good friends and later had very good lifelong relation, headmasterji helped dungermal gupta son Vinod gupta in studies – he took him to Agra specially to appear in the exams, provided tuitions to them. Headmasterji used to refer him as Dungerseth, Dungermal Gupta had high regards for his Guruji and he maintained it till death of Headmasterji. Household food grains used to come from Dungermal gupta's(Bilotia) shop from Surajgarh mandi.

Sevaramji gupta had helped the author of this book(by providing access to very old photos of Headmasterji at PB High School, Surajgarh).

Jugal Kishore Chawla (Retd. Income Tax Commissioner)

Jugal Kishore ji remembered Headmaster ji and said, "Rambilasji was my Guruji. I studied under him from Standard 3 to 10 in PB High School. I was his favourite student. He had always conferred his blessings on me. I attained the highest position in my profession and leading a successful & satisfied life. When I think about Headmasterji, three things that immediately strikes my mind are, first "Badhiya Insaan"(Nice human being), Second "Vidvaan" (Intellectual) and third Best teacher. I was from a very humble family and from a so-called Dalits at that time who would hardly be considered for education. It was because of Guruji's support, I could fight all those odds and could achieve higher Professional level. He even paid my fees for some years from his own salary without disclosing it to others. He usesd to guide me as his own son.

Headmasterji had a very good knowledge of Hindi, English, Sanskrit and Maths. He could narrate novel "Godaan" in such a lively manner that it seemed as if the story was being played right in front of our eyes. He would explain every character of Godaan, distinctly and clearly. With the same fluency he would narrate Shakespeare's play "Macbeth" and since it was English drama, after narrating the story, he would pick up difficult words and explain it to the students in Hindi. He helped us in participating in debates & Elocution. He would write the matter to be presented and then prepared the participant to deliver that. We always won such events. During his tenure as the headmaster of PB High School, Surajgarh witnessed many new initiatives. One of such events was Students Union Elections in 1955-56. One representative from each class was selected, who was named as the candidate for the Post of President of school union. There was no ballot system and students from class I-X were assembled in the hall and the candidates for election were made to stand in front. Rambilas ji & Rampratap ji monitored the process. The names of the candidates were called and the students were asked to raise their hands, if they supported the candidate. Shanti Joshi & I got the highest vote. Both of us were called on stage and Headmasterji asked me to support Shanti Joshi as the President of the union as, he was senior to me.

He published first School Newsletter in 1956, which was handwritten. He formed the team of eight people which included seven students with Mahaveer Prasad ji Khandelwal as Editor. The newsletters had the student achievements, talent corner for students, Teachers' opinion & write ups, poems, Essays, news etc." Jugal Kishore ji concluded by saying, "How much shall I tell you about Headmasterji, my words can't describe. I can only say, "Wo Sarva Guna Sampaanna the."

Chapter 13

Eventful Meetings with eminent people

Points covered

- **Sardar Vallabh Bhai Patel**
- **Lal Krishna Advani and BhaironSingh Shekhawat**
- **Guru Hanuman and Mahabali Satpal**
- **Vinoba Bhave and Pt. Jawahar lal Nehru**
- **Hajarilal Sharma-Chirawa**
- **GD Birla**
- **Ramkrishna Dalmia**
- **Seshram Ola**
- **Haribhau Upadhaya**
- **NarottamLal Joshi**

Chapter 13

Eventful Meetings with eminent people

Sardar Vallabh bhai Patel

Muhommad Ali Jinnah who was President of Muslim League was to speak to the workers in the Satluj Cotton Mills. In those days the staff of the Birlas at Satluj Cotton Mills were all Marwaris(Hindus from Pilani region of Rajasthan), and the supervisior and the workers were all Punjabi muslims, who were localites.

Jinnah instigated the workers by addressing, "All the workers at Sutluj cotton mills are Muslims and that is the reason why all of you are being paid lesser wages. You must stand up for higher wages. Birlas are not going to give heed to your demands easily and hence, you must declare strike." Hence the workers went on strike in the mill.

An example of this was the strike at Sutlej Cotton Mill. There were also labour shutdowns at Lyallpur Cotton Mills, the Okara Textile Mills and the Bata boot factory.

Hedmasterji was ware house incharge and workers agitating were putting stern demands in front of management. That was unacceptable. GD Birla was informed by Rambilasji Sharma about the strike and the attitude of the workers. GD spoke to Gandhiji, Nehru and other congressmen to intervene, since Satluj Cotton Mills was the largest mill in whole South East Asia in 1945. As the talks of partiions were already surfacing, no one was interested to go to Okara and pacify the workers; only Sarder Patel dared. Sardar Patel travelled all the way to Okara to break the strike. Sarder Patel was known to be an arch rightist, pro-capitalist, anti-labour, and extremely close to the Birlas. Gandhi and most other leaders (other than the two Nehrus), were also close to Birlas, but all of them, unlike Sardar Patel, maintained their distance from the Birlas. Around 1945, there was a strike in Birla Cotton Mills in Okara, which is now in Pakistan. Infact Sarder Patel threatened them all to withdraw the strike or else would starve for the food and shelters, even the Hindu workers supporting the strike were made clear that they would be jailed along with the Muslim workers.

Headmasterji had arranged the dinner for Sarder Patel. Headmasterji's brother in law-Mahavir Prasad Noondhwala-from Pilani was dairy and canteen incharge there in satluj cotton mills. Rambilasji had specialy ordered, and Sarder Patel asked Rambilasji to prepare for shifting back the families to native since the situation of the communal tension was grappling and partition was almost confirm. Sarder Patel even indicated Rambilasji-"You are so qualified and powerful orator, why don't you join politics." But Rambilasji politiely refused citing reasons of old parents and the sole responsibility of bread-earner for the family. Sarder said, "I will ask GD Birla to take you in some other concern in Hindustan." Rambilasji was quite thankful to Sardar for what sarder had done to save his job here, headmasterji had high regards for Sardar Patel.

Lal Krishna Advani & Bhairon Singh ji Shekhawat

RSS was initiated in Rajasthan in 1952-56. Lala Krishna Advani and Bhairon Singh Shekhawat were the grass root level Pracharak in Rajasthan. The strategy in those days was to find the influential person in a town or village, who was Hindu, educated and influenced youths to join RSS. And had a disciplined life.

Bhairon Singh Shekhawat came to Jhunjhunu and came to know that for Surajgarh, there was only one centre for school and educational activities, which had more than 1000 students from around 200 different villages.

The man incharge of PB high school was Headmaster ji Sh. Rambilas ji, who was very popular and the highly educated individual. Moreover he was acclaimed as the first graduate and first post graduate of Surajgarh in 1932 & 1936 respectively.

In the period immediately after independence, in 1947 & republic in 1950, there was only one party that was Congress, which had good hold in Jhunjhunu district. Sis Ram Ola was the young leader in Jhunjhunu Congress, GD Birla in Pilani and Master Hazari Lal Ji in Chirawa.

But Headmasterji was himself the victim of India-Pakistan Partition. His friend Vaidya Madan Lal ji Pushkarna and his Brother in Law, Mahavir Sharma (Noondwala-Pilani) and sister Godavari Devi were with him.

Headmasterji was a total non political, non controversial educational Leader in that region. But Born to a hindu Gaur Brahamin Parents, with an "Om" as birthmark embossed on his chest, was a hindu by heart. But he himself promoted many of his students to join Politics

The crux of the matter was that Lal Krishna Advani and Bhairon Singh Shekhawat were core hindus and RSS secretary(Lal Krishna Advani), started to work for Rajasthan from Alwar province and used to extensively visit Rajasthan and Shekhawati, as Bhairon Singh Shekhawat hailed from Khachariyawas, Sikar.

In one of their visits, Bhairon Singh ji and Advani ji met Headmasterji and even visited PB High School. Headmaster ji was very honest person and he said to Advani ji & Bhiaron singh ji that, "I am myself victim of Partition and it took me 8 days to reach Surajgarh from Lahore. My family had no hopes of my return." Bhairon Singh ji and Advani ji requested Headmaster ji to be incharge of RSS, Jhunjhunu district. Since, Headmasterji was heading an educational institution, he believed that he should be away from any politics, but he agreed to facilitate the formation and functioning of RSS –Shakha, Surajgarhby allowing them to address students who were interested in those activities of social work.

Rambilas ji and Political Thoughts

RSS was initiated in Rajasthan in 1952-56. Lala Krishna Advani and Bhairon Singh Shekhawat were the grass root level Pracharak in Rajasthan. The strategy in those days was to find the influential person in a town or village, who was Hindu, educated and influenced youths to join RSS. And had a disciplined life.

Bhairon Singh Shekhawat came to Jhunjhunu and came to know that for Surajgarh, there was only one centre for school and educational activities, which had more than 1000 students from around 200 different villages.

The man incharge of PB high school was Headmaster ji Sh. Rambilas ji, who was very popular and the highly educated individual. Moreover he was acclaimed as the first graduate and first post graduate of Surajgarh in 1932 & 1936 respectively.

In the period immediately after independence, in 1947 & republic in 1950, there was only one party that was Congress, which had good hold in Jhunjhunu district. Sis Ram Ola was the young leader in Jhunjhunu Congress, GD Birla in Pilani and Master Hazari Lal Ji in Chirawa.

But Headmasterji was himself the victim of India-Pakistan Partition. His friend Vaidya Madan Lal ji Pushkarna and his Brother in Law, Mahavir Sharma (Noondwala-Pilani) and sister Godavari Devi were with him.

Headmasterji was a total non political, non controversial educational Leader in that region. But Born to a hindu Gaur Brahamin Parents, with an "Om" as birthmark embossed on his chest, was a hindu by heart. But he himself promoted many of his students to join Politics

The crux of the matter was that Lal Krishna Advani and Bhairon Singh Shekhawat were core hindus and RSS secretary(Lal Krishna Advani), started to work for Rajasthan from Alwar province and used to extensively visit Rajasthan and Shekhawati, as Bhairon Singh Shekhawat hailed from Khachariyawas, Sikar.

In one of their visits, Bhairon Singh ji and Advani ji met Headmasterji and even visited PB High School. Headmaster ji was very honest person and he said to Advani ji & Bhiaron singh ji that, "I am myself victim of Partition and it took me 8 days to reach Surajgarh from Lahore. My family had no hopes of my return." Bhairon Singh ji and Advani ji requested Headmaster ji to be incharge of RSS, Jhunjhunu district. Since, Headmasterji was heading an educational institution, he believed that he should be away from any politics, but he agreed to facilitate the formation and functioning of RSS –Shakha, Surajgarh.

Most of the people were scared to join RSS, as Congress ruled the country. To encourage Hinduism and National self -help, headmasterji convened the speech in PB High School ground with all students His nephew Hari Ram Ghagshyan took the students and other youth to RSS Shakha. Headmasterji's son, Savita Prakash ji, who was 11 years then, also joined the RSS activities.

Others like Jugal Kishore Khatik, Mahavir Khandelwal, Hiralal Joshi, Satyaprakash Sharma, Murlidhar Badraika and many other joined in and that was how RSS Shakha became functional.(This was narrated by one of the headmasterji's student-Jugal kishore Khatig in an interview conducted at jaipur.)

Dungarmal Gupta and Saligram Gupta, who were in Surajgarh mandi, helped the shakha financially.

RSS then started in Backdoor in Surajgarh in 1950.RSS after 1960, started spreading its root gradually in Surajgarh. The Water distribution at Surajgarh railway station by RSS activitists use to shout on railway plat form in standing train "hindu pani"(water for hindus.). many of the senior in Surajgarh who were in teens in those days still remembers this.

Headmasterji clearly conveyed that he wanted the development of society at large for Surajgarh. Hence, he considered the opportunity to support RSS, as the development of the youth of Surajgarh as the volunteers (Swayam Sevak), so that they could in turn facilitate the all-round development of society. This was the need of an hour, as post-independence the society was in tatters. RSS then started in Backdoor in Surajgarh in 1950.RSS after 1960, started spreading its root gradually in Surajgarh. The Water distribution at Surajgarh railway station by RSS activitists use to shout on railway platform in stationary train "hindu pani"(water for hindus.). Headmasterji only took this as an opportunity to serve society and selfhelp. Many of the seniors in Surajgarh who were in their teens in those days still remember this.

Bhairon Singh ji frequently visited Surajgarh and stayed at Dungarmal Gupta's residence in Surajgarh Mandi. This was due to the request that Gupta ji made to Headmaster ji, that he would like to host them. (the information is confirmed by Shri. Sevaram gupta- son of late Dungermal gupta)

RAMBILASJI AND GURU HANUMAN- THE GREAT WRESTLER (Padmshree -1983, Dronacharya Award For Wrestling 1984) AND MAHABALI SATPAL 1982 GOLD MEDALIST FOR WRESTLING

Headmasterji has been a promotor of sports also and had very close terms with Wrestler, Guru Hanuman of Chirawa. Guru Hanuman is a reciepient of Dronacharya award for Coaching in 1988 and Padma Shree in 1983.

Guru Hanuman Akhara that comes under Wrestling Federation of India was established in 1925 in the space of Birla cotton mills in new delhi, Shri murlidhar Dalmia(friend of Rambilasji and from Surajgarh) was and is the epicenter of the ancient wrestling tradition in India. It is the oldest akhara existing in India till now located at Shakti Nagar in New Delhi that has produced National and International wrestlers for India.

Guru Hanuman Akhara has produced wrestlers like Dara Singh, Guru Satpal, Sushil Kumar, Yogendra Kumar, Anuj Chowdhary, Rajiv Tomer, Anil Mann, Sujit Mann, Naveen, Rakesh Goonga and many others.

The club was named after the legendary Indian wrestler, Guru Hanuman, who was born in Chirawa village in 1901 in Western Rajasthan. Hanuman was awarded the Padma Shri, one of India's highest civilian honours and he was the recipient of the Shree Dronacharya Award, a prize named after the mythical sage warrior which is reserved for sports coaches. Hanuman died in a car accident at Partapur, Meerut in 1999.

More than 100 boys are enrolled and some are outstation students coming from different states of India that live in the akhara. The boys have been divided into teams and each team is given the responsibility of cleaning, cooking, washing, and other jobs. Once the boys get over with their wrestling exercises, they have to do rest of the household chores.

Picture Reference 42: *Headmasterji has been a promotor of sports also and had very close terms with Wriestling Guru Hanuman-from Chirawa. In the photograph, headmasterji is seen with Wriestling Guru Hanuman-reciepient of Dronacharya award for Coaching, and padmbhusan in 1982. also seen in the photograph is Asiad olympic wriestling gold medalist Satpal(extreme left.).satpal Olympic silver jeetne wale sushil kumar ke guru or sasur h.*

YEAR 1958-60
RAMBILASJI AND VISIT OF VINOBA BHAVE AT SURAJGARH

SAINT VINOBA BHAVE IN 1940 WAS CHOSEN AS First satyagrahi against bristish rule.

It is said that even gandhiji envied and respected vinoba's celebracy.

Vinoba bhave also participated in the quit India movement. Vinoba observed the life of the average Indian living in a village and tried to find solution for the problem he faced, with firm spiritual foundation.

This formed the core of his public movement-SARVODAY movement(awakening of all potential). He believed in Sarvodaya = welfare of all through, science + spirituality

Another example of this is the famous –Bhoodan andolan- (donate land for poor). He travelled across in villages for almost 14 years and walking 70,000 kms. He receieved seventeen lac hectares of land donation for the landless farmers. During his 14 year long travel across india he asked the people with excessive land- if you have five sons, treat me as your 6 th son and give me one-sixth part of the land as gift, later vinoba distributed the gifted land to the landless farmers- to create balance and help the poor to do farming, and support livelihood of their family.

Non violence and compassion being hallmark of his philosophy, he also carried campaigns against the slaughtering of cow, and the activists surrounded the parliament house.

Saint Vinoba bhave was a scholar, thinker and a writer. His over all contribution for the people fetch him the first Ramon Magsasay award in 1958. And Bharat ratna in 1983.

Saint vinoba was very popular and started his movements in those days. He started the visit of Rajasthan. During his visit to jhunjhunu district- he was accompanied by many including -Janki devi bajaj- wife of famous freedom fighter Jamnalal bajaj.

Picture Reference 43: Vinoba Bhave in Surajgarh, 1959

Picture Reference 44: Pandit Jawahar Lal Nehru with Vinoba Bhave during Bhoodan Andolan in Surajgarh

Picture Reference 45: Unique Guard of Honour to Vinoba Bhave by Students of PB High School-Surajgarh year-1959-60.

Head masterji was president of Shri Krishna parishad and principal of PB high school.

Vinoba bhave had visited to jhunjhunu, chirawa, pilani and then Surajgarh. From Surajgarh he went to Haryana.

Saint vinoba bhave was accompanied by forty people including -Smt. Janaki devi Bajaj(w/o Jamnalal Bajaj), Narottamlal Joshi-First speaker of the Rajasthan Assembly (1952-57)-official representative of state government of rajasthan, Hajarilal Sharma-MLA-chirawa, B.V.Keshkar(IB- minister in 1959-60)-official representative of government of india.

Under his guidance, In 1960, All India Radio was the only truly national organisation that reached and touched everybody. Pandit **Ravi Shankar** even composed the signature tune for AIR. The national programmes produced great concerts by great musicians. Every other Saturday, Hindustani and Carnatic musicians would play jugalbandis, bridging a gap that had existed for many long years.

"The then IB minister, **B.V. Keskar**, restricted the playing of Hindi film music on AIR, so then Radio Ceylon swamped the airwaves with Binaca Geetmala—a hit parade of film songs—broadcast by **Hameed** and **Ameen Sayani**. Keskar had to allow film music back and the Vividh Bharati channel was created. TV was some years away—although the first experimental broadcast of Doordarshan took place in 1959, regular service only started by 1965. By 1967, TV was important enough that Mr.Malik hosted a show on it with Marlon Brando and Satyajit Ray.

Even The speech given by Sant vinoba Bhave in Surajgarh and the introductory speech given by Rambilasji Headmasterji and trailing speech by narrotamlal Joshi and BV Keshkar were broadcasted under the talks of sant vinoba Bhave. Very few people know about this. infact Headmasterji is the only person in the history of Surajgarh whose words got aired at AIR, courtesy IB minister-BV Keshkar.

Coming back to vinoba bhave Surajgarh visit, the Surajgarh swagat samiti was made of Rambilasji Sharma- president of the Shrikrishna parishad and Principal of PB high School, Babulalji agarwal, Babulal choudhary, Tulsiram shah, Madanlal pushkarna, Mahavirprasad Sharma- Surajgarh municipality member and others active members of the Surajgarh were key persons to welcome saint vinoba bhave and his associates for his bhodan andolan. And were ready with flowers and garland.

The vinoba team came from pilani from deroad, entered from road from police station, old bus stop to chokario bazaar- there was no Gandhi statue in the Surajgarh market. and a big open plot in front parishad bhavan. hundreds of people had gathered on both side of road including 400 students of pb high school from the route of the historical boodan andolan-around the way vinoba bhave was supposed to pass through, except 50 student involved in official function. Other official members of the committee were given the responsibility of guiding the members of vinoba team to PB high school.

Vinoba's slogan was "Jai Jagat"

He was travelling whole of India barefoot for his mission-"bhoodan andolan". Vinoba bhave was Brahmin and he was very happy to see rambilasji Sharma – who was principal of the PB high school and chairman of the shri Krishna parishad, he told Headmasterji – you and I both are Brahmin by cast and are imparting our free service for all lower and upper cast of the society. One day when the society will be well to do, Surajgarh will remember you, your effort for the promotion of the education. headmasterji was pioneer for that in Surajgarh. He also told vinobaji that he is probably the first graduate and postgraduate of Surajgarh. Upon which vinoba took out his garland

and honoured haeadmasterji. This was probably the first public honour of "the first graduate and first post graduate of Surajgarh,."(unfortunately the family could not preserve the photograh of the historic event).

In those days lower cast people used to work as bonded labourers in farms. Vinoba bhave conveyed in his speech to all land lords-" if you have five son, treat me as 6th son and donate me 1/6th of your land, which I will transfer to the poor bonded labourers, so that he can farm and take care of his family and be self reliant.

Saint vinoba bhave knew that PB high school was one of the biggest school in Surajgarh area, including 100 villages under it. there were around 400-500 students. Rambilas Sharma-Headmasterji was key to unlock all those thousands young mind and convey them about bhoodan andolan. Upon entry of Vinoba Bhave – there was a huge cry of slogan- jai jagat, jay vinoba by students.

Headmasterji has arranged a unique honour at pb high school, around hundreds of student created a guard of honour with sticks in the sky in pairs –continously by making a welcome gate. The old villagers still remembers this from their student age. Vinoba was very happy by the grand reception from students and Headmasterji –rambilasji Sharma.

Students were very curious about autograph of vinoba bhave. But on looking at the huge numbers of students, Smt. jankidevi bajaj intervined and came with and idea to sort out few students out of hundreds of students standing there. She said '- baba, gandhiji takes Rs.5 from each person for his autograph. Because there would be very few students to pay sRs.5/- for an autograph, and thus the crowd would sortout,.

But vinobaji replied-" gandhiji is a mahajan, he may have love for money, but I am a Brahmin, my dharm say to impart it free. Janakidevi immediately could not react to it. infact he had no world.

Sant vinoba gave the autograph along with name of the student, to as many as he could. Rambilasji's son –Savitaprakash Sharma was one of the lucky student to get the autograph.

Vinoba 's speech was all about his mission- in the thank u speech Headmasterji addressed the need fo education especially in the lower faction of society. He emphasized on need of saving girl child and education girls.

After the speech, the members of the andolan were offered snacks ihgand tea and vinoba bhave did not took any thing to eat, for he had ulser in his stomach, so he used to take only chass- water of the curd. He took it from the hands of one of the students – Savitaprakash Sharma who was merely 15 yrs of age then. The autograph is the testimony.

This event was recorded in the history of Surajgarh.

Headmasterji has asked the student in those years in 1959-60 in exams – to write a prose on bhoodan andolan, and thus was inculcating the ideas spread by Vinoba Bhave.

Ghanshyam Das Birla

Rambilasji returned to Surajgarh in 1936. The same year his eldest son, Sh. Omprakash ji was born. Rambilas ji joined Chirawa high school as a teacher. He had good command over English, because of his education from the best institutes. He had charismatic voice. In those days GD Birla, had a discussion with his father in law, Mahadeo ji Somany, emphasizing on the need of strengthening English of the people of Shekhawati. The school annual function was organized to encourage the students and boost their potential. The educational leaders and the Industrialists were invited as the Chief Guest and the Guest of Honor. This was one of occasion where the students' performance could bring name, fame and reputation to the school and hence would increase the employability of the children. As a coordinator, Rambilas ji got the opportunity to address the students in one of these functions, where he chooses to speak in English. The chief guest was Sh. GD Birla, who was impressed to hear the speech of Rambilas ji and congratulated him for that. This was the first occasion when Rambilasji met GD Birla.

There after, GD Birla called him to discuss his relocation to Okara for the job at Birla School, Okara, Lahore.

Rambilasji and Hajarilal Sharma-MLA, Chirawa

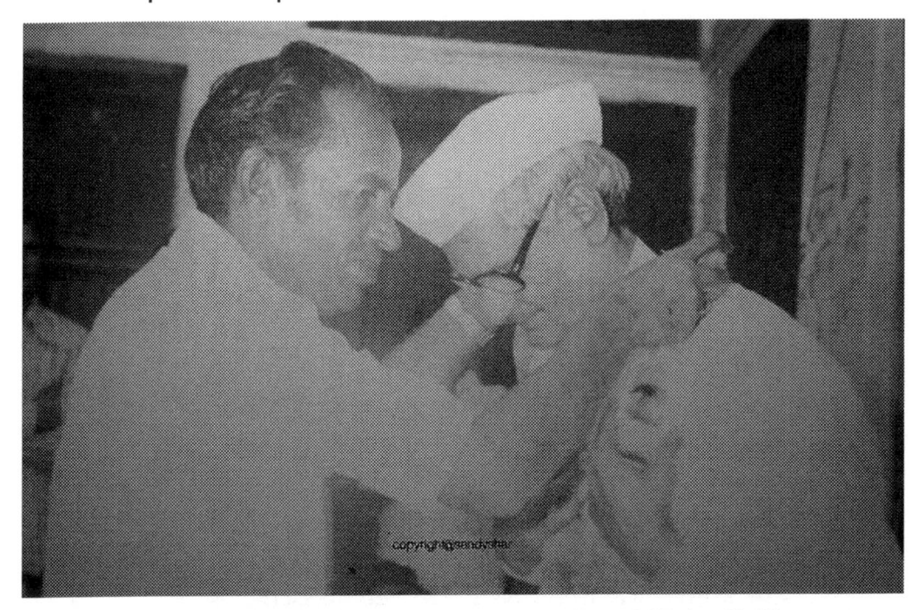

Picture reference 46: Headmasterji and Hajarilalji during election campaign in Surajgarh

Rambilasji Sharma had good relation with Hajarilal Sharma-MLA for three terms from Chirawa.

As per Hajarlalji,(during the meeting at chirawa and jaipur with the author) had narrated that Rambilasji Headmasterji had been senior to him at Chirawa high school right from the year 1938 and was gem of a person. He had very good command over English and mathematics both. He was first graduate and then postgraduate in the history of Surajgarh from Lahore university, which was an honour in those days. He taught in the Chirawa high school upto 1943. He was non political, non controversial personality in that region and had high regards in education circle. He preferred to serve his village and develop education there though he had receieved many good offers as head/ director/principal of very repute including BITS- pilani. Surajgarh should never forget his contribution in education field. Even during my political career as MLA I had met Headmasterji many times and always regarded him as my elder and his mother as my Bhuaji, as she hails from a very good family of chirawa.

Later in year 2002 Hajarilalji's granddaughter Dr.Ekta Sharma (daughter of Sunderlal Sharma-RPS) got married to Sandeep Sharma(Grandson of Rambilasji Headmasterji,) and the author of this book and the legacies still continues.

Headmasterji and Sisram Ola-(Cabinet minister in Government of India from congress till December 2013.) (Mentioned in the Earlier Chapter)

Haribhau Upadhaya-Education minister of Rajasthan-1966

Haribhau Upadhaya was education minister under in Mohanlal Sukhadia ministry. He ryoften visited PB high School on 15th August and 26th January celebration and Flag march. He was a very good friend of Headmasterji. upon one such visit in 1966, how Headmasterji had helped one of the students overcome his stage fear. The student narrated to the author and its account is as given under.

Shri Omkar Agarwal of Surajgarh Mandi, passed class X in 1966, he narrated, "I was shy and introvert. Headmasterji wanted me to participate in debate competition. I went to Headmasterji and confessed that I did not know what to speak, how to speak and would not be able to withstand the gathering. I won't be able to utter a single word. I am not confident. Listening to this, headmasterji did not give up rather gave personal coaching to me and wrote a debate script for me and made sure that I practice the debate in front of mirror. His motivation gave me courage and I stood second in the competition. It was indeed a great pleasure to receive the certificate from the hands of Shri Haribhau Upadhyay, then Education Minister of Rajasthan, who has come to host flag on 15th august in 1966. This boosted my confidence and changed me for the life time. I still remember what he said about Headmasterji in his speech that the young generation was fortunate enough to have Rambilas ji as their guide, teacher and philosopher. It was sure that wherever these students would go they would shine and excel in whatever they do. It was not because of a system but because of an incarnation of God and true educationalist- Rambilasji. I pay my gratitude to Rambilas ji for the successful life as a business man."

PART VI

RAMBILAS JI'S PERSONA

Chapter 14

Rambilas ji's philosophy of life

Points covered

- **Rambilasji's essence of life and its reflections**
- **Impact of Swami Vivekananda**
- **Rambilasji's beliefs & thoughts**
- **Rambilasji and Political thought**
- **Headmaster ji a diligent**

Chapter 14

Rambilas ji's philosophy of life

Rambilasji's essence of life and its reflection

Headmasterji personality is still visible by following words.
OM- his belief
Satya- belief in truth
Savitaprakash- the Sun and Sunshine- he believed in only worshipping sun god and daily offering water to sun.
Sajjan- character he had.
Suniti- believe in good policy
Gayatri- The shakti and strength within every individual.
He named his six children – Om Prakash, Satya Prakash, Savitaprakash, Sajjan, Suniti and Gayatri. These names reflects his philosophy of life.

i.e. A man believe in Om - the ultimate god., always be truthful, spread light of education like the sun spread the light and warmth, be humble, always work on the good policies and got connected to gayatri as his shakti in the end of life.

Impact of Swami Vivekanada Ji

Head masterji was greatly influenced by Swami Vivekanand right from his childhood. He had visited Khetri and liked the place where Narendra Dutta became Swami Vivekanand in Khetri.

In year 1897, Vivekananda wrote to Swami Akhandananda, "Go from door to door amongst the poor and lower classes of the town of Khetri and teach them religion. Also, let them have oral lessons on geography and such other subjects."

Headmasterji had a great influence of Swami Vivekanand and had clear understanding that he had to take the mission of literacy for Surajgarh. Education would be an important asset for the freedom fighters and for all in Surajgarh even immediately after independence.

From young age itself Headmasterji had decided to devote himself for this cause.

Rambilasji's belief and thoughts

In his first speech at PB High School, headmasterji, spoke his mind and talked about his thoughts and beliefs regarding education. He emphasized on learning all the aspects, to develop the nation. He motivated and envisioned his students to reach the global stature. Excerpt of the speech is as follows: "The world is transient, so it is important and essential to have change in every walk of life, with the changing world. Those who cannot match the pace with the changing times, they are at loss. Along with the traditional courses like Sanskrit, literature etc., it is also important to introduce the new and modern subjects and topics of science to the students, to prepare them for the contemporary times and be successful. Today because of the science, there has been enlightenment in the world. We should put in our best efforts to attain that expertise. The inventions of Western world-Europe and America, cannot be neglected and ignored. We need to know and understand them. It is important to study and know the History of all nations, and Compare the culture and civilization of one country to another so that we can develop the spirit of competition and lead the other countries in development. Our country is agriculture intensive. Knowledge of agricultural science needs deep understanding of the geography of the place, so knowledge of the geography of the world is equally important as the knowledge of Science. Similarly, knowledge of the global language, English, National Language, Hindi and Language of practical applications, mathematics are equally important."

This speech was not the mere words but Rambilas ji had lived them throughout his life. He had Post graduation degree in English, Hindi and Sanskrit. He himself had a degree of ayurvedacharya and Sahitya Ratna as well. He also had degree in Mathematics. So, it was not only preaching but leading by example.

Rambilas ji and Political Thoughts

RSS was initiated in Rajasthan in 1952-56. Lala Krishna Advani and Bhairon Singh Shekhawat were the grass root level Pracharak in Rajasthan. The strategy in those days was to find the influential person in a town or village, who was educated and influenced youths to join RSS. And had a disciplined life.

Bhairon Singh Shekhawat came to Jhunjhunu and came to know that for Surajgarh, there was only one centre for school and educational activities, which had influended more than 1000 students from around 200 different villages.

The man incharge/architect of PB high school was Headmaster ji Sh. Rambilas ji, who was very popular and the highly educated individual. Moreover he was acclaimed as the first graduate and first post graduate of Surajgarh in 1932 & 1936 respectively. further L K Advaniji got to know that Rambilasji Sharma studied at GCU- Lahore. Advaniji was personally very pleased to meet Rambilasji, both had their own struggle stories / experiences of pain and likelihood about Lahore and karanchi.

In the period immediately after independence, in 1947 & republic in 1950, there was only one party that was Congress, which had good hold in Jhunjhunu district. Sis Ram Ola was the young leader in Jhunjhunu Congress, GD Birla in Pilani and Master Hazari Lal Ji in Chirawa.

But Headmasterji was himself the victim of India-Pakistan Partition. His friend Vaidya Madan Lal ji Pushkarna and his Brother in Law, Mahavir Sharma (Noondwala-Pilani) and sister Godavari Devi were with him.

Headmasterji was a total non political, non controversial educational Leader in that region. But Born to a hindu Gaur Brahamin Parents, with an "Om" as birthmark embossed on his chest, was a hindu by heart. But he himself promoted many of his students to join Politics

The crux of the matter was that Lal Krishna Advani and Bhairon Singh Shekhawat were core hindus and RSS secretary(Lal Krishna Advani), started to work for Rajasthan from Alwar province and used to extensively visit Rajasthan and Shekhawati, as Bhairon Singh Shekhawat hailed from Khachariyawas, Sikar in early fifties.

In one of their visits, Bhairon Singh ji and Advani ji met Headmasterji and even visited PB High School. Headmaster ji was very honest person and he said to Advani ji & Bhiaron singh ji that, "I am myself victim of Partition and it took me 8 days to reach Surajgarh from Lahore. My family had no hopes of my return." Bhairon Singh ji and Advani ji requested Headmaster ji to be incharge of RSS, Jhunjhunu district. Since, Headmasterji was heading an educational institution, he believed that he should be away from any politics, but he agreed to facilitate the formation and functioning of RSS –Shakha, Surajgarh.

Most of the people were scared to join RSS, as Congress ruled the country. To encourage Hinduism and National self -help, headmasterji convened the speech in PB High School ground with all students His nephew Hari Ram Ghagshyan took the students and other youth to RSS Shakha. Headmasterji's son, Savita Prakash ji, who was 11 years then, also joined the RSS activities.

Others like Jugal Kishore Khatik, Mahavir Khandelwal, Hiralal Joshi, Satyaprakash Sharma, Murlidhar Badraika and many other joined in and that was hoe RSS Shakha became functional.

Dungarmal Gupta and Saligram Gupta, who were in Surajgarh mandi, helped the shakha financially.

RSS then started in Backdoor in Surajgarh in 1950.RSS after 1960, started spreading its root gradually in Surajgarh.

Bhairon Singh ji frequently visited Surajgarh and stayed at Dungarmal Gupta's residence in Surajgarh Mandi. This was due to the request that Gupta ji made to Headmaster ji, that he would like to host them.

RSS activities would serve water and food on the railway station of Surajgarh and would refer to it as "Hindu Pani".

Later on Headmasterji did not join any political activities till he served as principal in PB high school, till 1971, after his retirement in 1972-75, again JP andolan was active and emergency was declared in 1975.

The Jan Sangh, later Janta Party was launched in Surajgarh, and Rambilas ji headmasterji, was unanimously elected head of Janta Party, Surajgarh unit. Head amster ji gave the speech in chokario Bazar, and people still remember the charismatic words of Headmasterji. Even during the speech Rambilas ji asked them to elect someone else, since he was not keeping well in 1975-76. He had kidney problem. Babulal ji Halwai, Babulal ji Chaudhary, Dungarmal Gupta, Saligram Gupta, Madan lal Pushkarna were among key people. Unfortunately, Headmasterji, due to his ailing health, could not continue with these activities. In 1976 he was bed-ridden and in 1977 he passed away.

But it is evident that the golden chapters of RSS, Jan Sangh, janta Party and BJP, were written by him In Surajgarh. Today BJP stands tall in Surajgarh and the MP from Surajgarh Smt. Santosh Ahlawat won by tremendous votes, but truth remains that headmasterji is still "NEEV KA PATHAR".

Because his selfless service to people, Natives of Surajgarh remembers him fondly even today.

In 1957, after the independence, the state legislation elections were contested in Surajgarh. Sis Ram Ola Ji was the contestant from the joint seat of Khetri- Surajgarh. During the convassing, Sis Ram ji came to Surajgarh along with Hazari Lal ji masterji and Mahavir Prasad ji Sharma(EX Chairman). All three of them had a consensus that Ram Bilas ji was the most influential person of Surajgarh. So they decided to meet Rambilas ji and hence went to his home. Everybody knew that Headmaster ji respected her mother the most, so it would be better to meet his mother. All of them reached headmasterji's house. hazari lal ji used to address Headmasterji's mother as "Bua", as she was sister of Isar das ji Sehal of Chirawa. He greeted her. Then Mahaveer Prasad ji and Sis ram j I bowed. Headmasterji's mother giving blessings to Sis ram ji said, "Jeevto Reh, beta". On this Ola ji insisted," Maa, chunav mein jeet to reh. Yo aashirwaad do". On this maa replied, "Chokho bhaya, Chunav mein bhi jeet to reh". In the mean time Headmasterji came out and all three of them touched his feet. Sis ram ji said, "Headmaster ji maa to chunav jitney ko aashirwad de chuki hai, baki kaam tharo hai. Sab thare pe hai" Hence, headmaster ji replied, "Jud maa hi aashirwad de diyo hai, to mein kyan mana kar saku hun. Mero bhi sahayog aur aashirwad thare saath hai".

This was the first chapter of Educated Politics in Surajgarh. There were only two centres where people gathered- Shri Krishna Parishad and PB High School. The members of Sri Krishna Parishad, were the alumni of PB High school. Hence the centre of both the places was Shri Ram Bilas ji and ola ji received the blessings for his first electoral win.

Head master ji- A Diligent

1956-57

Picture Reference 47: Headmasterji

Headmaster ji, was principal of the school and was diligent. He did all his work on his own. He would come straight from school to home, would go to farm and look after the chores there, and if needed would also do that.

He has reached the heights in his educational career. He was a genious. He was such a good teacher that students would go to him after the school at home to learn from him and if would find him doing some work, would start helping him in that.

In 1956-57, Ramswaroop, son of Nandmal Halwai and Kothimal of mandi would go to Headmasterji's house for free tuitions but headmaster ji did not refuse education to anybody. If they would not find them home they would go walking to the headmasterji's farm, which was 6 kilometre from there. So students did not mind walking extra 12 kilometres to learn from him.

The students respected headmasterji a lot and despite the fact that headmaster ji would never ask any of his student to help him in personal chores, the students loved fetching water to his house, feeding the cows in Nohra etc.

Chapter 15

Rambilasji as Social Reformer

Points covered

- **As an educational reformer**
- **Women educationalist**
- **Social and Family Reformer**
- **Infrastructure reforms for Village development**
- **NCC & Sports**
- **Agriculture, trade and industrialisation @ Surajgarh**

Chapter 15

Rambilasji as Social Reformer

Rambilas ji introduced Education reforms in school days. He introduced English in class 3 from year 1950. He initiated his social reforms through Shri Krishna Parishad. Activities like library, All India Radio news listening centre, TV in library, dance, ramleela, dramas, skits, comedy, and sports events were started by inspiration of Headmasterji.

Rambilas ji as educational reformist of Surajgarh

Picture Reference 48: Headmasterji standing Seventh from left during felicitation ceremony of Indradev Pandey (Guruji of Headmasterji).

Rambilas ji was firm believer in setting own examples and then persuading others to follow. If he would give some advice to others, he would first do it and then convey it to others. He was self-motivated to upgrade education.

He was an avid learner and kept studying till the end of his life. He believed that continuous improvisation is the best thing for an individual in all aspects of life.

He persuaded people around him to learn. He himself continued studies.

Friends: He was a continuous source of inspiration. He encouraged his friends- Matadin ji, Madan lal ji Pushkarna (Vaidya) and many more to study further.

Son & Daughter: He pushed his sons to study and earn degrees. The era when women education was a taboo, he made his daughter study and also made her clear the "Vidhya Vinodini" Exam which used to be equivalent to secondary examination in those days

Daugter in laws-
His Relatives
His students
His colleagues
Parents of his students
Hence, he influenced the whole society

Women Education and Empowerment

Women Education
Literacy rate in India – during 60's and 70's
18.33 per cent in 1951,28.30 per cent in 1961, 34.45 per cent in 1971, 43.57 per cent in 1981

Literacy Rate - India: 1951-1991

Year	Persons	Male	Female
1951	18.33	27.16	8.86
1961	28.30	40.39	15.33
1971	34.45	45.95	21.97
1981	43.57	56.38	29.76
	(41.43)	(53.46)	(28.47)
1991	52.21	64.13	39.23

http://www.teindia.nic.in/mhrd/50yrsedu/y/3T/9U/3T9U0301.htm

Women literacy rate
Urban-Rural Differential in Literacy

Rates - INDIA: 1961-91

Year	Age group	Literacy Rate Urban Areas	Literacy Rate Rural Areas	Difference in rural/urban areas (% age points)
1961	5 and over	54.43	22.46	31.97
1971	5 and over	60.22	27.89	32.33
1981*	5 and over	64.85	34.04	30.81
1981*	7 and over	67.20	36.00	31.20
1981**	7 and over	73.08	44.69	28.39

Status of Women in Indian society

Efforts of Headmasterji towards boosting women education

The literacy rate was quite low in 1950's. If we observe the data the women literacy rate was abysmal. The status of women was ignoble and hence she was deprived of many important facilities and services eg.

Education. The girl's got married at early age and the parents' were not in favour of girl's education. She was taught to confine herself to the four walls of the house and learn home chores only. Contrary to today's time, father and daughter bonding was very restricted. The father would not interact with his daughter after certain age. It was to reinforce her that she needs to maintain distance from males. It was highly patriarchal society.

Women Education in Post -Independence Era was in very bad shape & especially in Rajasthan. At that time, Rambilas ji would always inspire vaniks and financially well-off people to come forward and contribute for the cause of women education.

He himself sent her daughter to the school from 1948-58, when the girls were not sent to school. As her daughter Smt. Gayatri Devi Dhand commemorates, "There were only 4 girls in the school. Besides me, Draupadi, Sajjan Pujari's daughter Sushila and Ratni Gilluram Bharatia could get the chance to study".

At the time when father would not interact with the daughter, would not allow her to study and would not sit next to each other; you can imagine what would be the condition of daughter in laws. Nobody could think of a situation when father in law and daughter in law are sitting together and talking. It was a taboo.

But Headmaster ji did not allow such taboos to be hurdle in his ways to educate his family. This distinguished Headmasterji from rest of his cohorts and contemporaries. He had five sons and he made all five daughter –in-laws to, in one or the other way, attain some educational level. He persuaded all the women in his family to appear in the exam of "Vidhya Vinodini", which was equivalent to secondary examination and in those days, this was the qualification required to be a primary school teacher. Her youngest daughter in law, Smt. Santosh, took the training in nursing and made it her career.

He would even allow his "Daughter in Laws" to sit in his classes, which he used to organize for the students who needed extra guidance. At the time of "Purda system", he would defy it and would consider her as another student, He would buy books for them, write question and answers to facilitate learning and prepare for exams. This was not all. But in those days for the undergraduation examination, students had to go to Agra to take the exam and there was no other centre of examination. Hence, the daughter- in -laws had to go to Agra, to write the exam. But this did not stop headmaster ji to encourage his daughter- in –laws to pursue higher education, rather he would accompany them to Agra for the exam and would also make the arrangements for the stay during examination days.

He may be considered as a "deviant", as he deviated from the societal norms of those times, by allowing his daughter in laws to not only study but also take employment, as a result they were all independent and were the symbol of "Women Empowerment". An Empowered individual would be one who experiences a sense of confidence & self -worth; a person who critically analyse his/her social and political environment, a person who is able to exercise control over decisions that affect his/her life. As education would empower an individual, efforts of Headmaster ji were geared towards "Women empowerment".

"The Desire to Educate, never came to an end, till headmaster ji's life ended"

Infrastructure reforms for Village development

Headmaster ji believed that development of any place is basically development of political, economic, social, technological, legal and environmental development. And key to all these development is "Education".

We need to educate people about basic requirements of life in Surajgarh. The political leadership should address this issue.

Headmasterji himself was apolitical, but he understood that development of political leadership was inevitable. So he promoted all his students towards debates, social activities, NCC camps, Sports competition, to encourage team spirit and competitiveness.

In sports, Football was his favourite game and continuous flow of energy and fighting spirit are the essence of this game. Headmaste ji wanted to nurture and groom these qualities amongst his students. Rambilas ji knew that life in small village like Surajgarh would require continuous struggle to achieve its goal and the struggle should come from the educated youth brigade of Surajgarh.

So education was his weapon of empowerment.

Agriculture Trade & Industrialization @Surajgarh

Agricultural reforms – In those days only from bajra, jowar, moong, moth were grown in Surajgarh. After coming back to Surajgarh, Rambilas ji discussed with the farmers about the scope to sow chana. As chana was not sown in Surajgarh before 1932. Rambilas ji had seen the crop of chana in Lahore Punjab. He thought that this would help in setting up Dal mills and would increase employment opportunities and develop the region. Chana production gave opportunities for industrialisation of Surajgarh- by setting Dal mills.

In one time there was highest no. of dal mills inSurajgarh in Rajasthan.

At Okarra, Montgomery, Punjab (now in Pakistan) the Britishers had started the dairy industry had flourished well. Headmasterji knew that the religious feeling for cow in Surajgarh, can easily have cow care taking centres, infact the cattle feed for cow will not be a problem and hence he suggested a unique model for the cooperative dairy industry, where cow would be taken care, the fooder would come from the money donated for the religious feeling people had for cow and this could give rise to a cooperative dairy industry- dealing in milk, ghee, curd, buttermilk, Sweets like peda and even icecreams. The project was good but some how could not click, but the gaushalas started... so the first step towards dairy industries was taken by Rambilasji Sharma. Moreover the bulls could be lent to the farmers for farming at a very reasonable rate. Hence would lend a helping hand to farming.

Metal industries had developed in nearby villages covered under surajgarh-eg. Metal producing and utensil manufacturing small scale enterpreneurs used to flourish near Loha-ru, (the name it self indicates lohar –means blacksmith and town of blacksmiths) availability of the metals like iron, copper, zinc, etc was easily available and hence good industries were developed.

Government of india's "Hindustan Zinc ltd (copper projects) at Khetri is probably biggest industry near surajgarh. Trade and commerece was very well developed in surajgarh mandi(the chamber of commerece and trade at suragarh),

Surajgarh even use to exports food, edibles to Burma, china, Nepal, Bhutan, Pakistan, afganistan, Iraq, Iran and other gulf countries etc.

NCC and Sports

Picture Reference 49: NCC cadets of Jhunjhunu district with Headmasterji

NCC was established in the year 1948 and started its wings in different states by 1950.

Picture Reference 50: ACC Social Camp at Kota, by PB High School cadets

Kusti or wrestling as a sports in jhunjhunu

Picture Reference 51: Headmasterji with Muralidhar Dalmiya

PB HIGH SCHOOL- PRINCIPAL DAYS – GOLDEN ERA OF PB SCHOOL

Picture Reference 52: PB High School staff

Standing 1st row: Mulidhar Badrika, Ramesh-Science Teacher, Mahavirji Khandelval

2nd Row Standing: Devkaran Singh-Sports, Second Unknown, Panji Master, Shyamji-Science Teacher, Hanumanprasad Jat- Accounts, Rameshwar Dayal Sharma(Pilod)

3rd Row: Sitting: Shivnarayan Shastri, Banvarilal Sharma(Bod), Rambilas Sharma-Principal, Panalal Modi(Drawing Teacher), Murlidhar Joshi-Hindi.

Chapter 16

Characteristics of Rambilas ji

Points covered

- **Love for friends**
- **Teach his children**
- **Self-respect**
- **Patient teacher**
- **Pitra paksha ekadashi and Rambilasji's love for his forefathers**
- **Good Human Being**

Chapter 16

Characteristics of Rambilas ji

Rambilas ji as a visionary

Visionary is a person with original ideas about what the future will and could be like. They are persistent, open and strategic planners. Rambilaji stood out as a visionary. He was persistent, open, strategic planner and also an idealistic.

Persistent: Rambilas ji pursued higher education and had earned MA in Sanskrit, English and Hindi. He exhibited his persistence to obtain higher education. He came back from Lahore after partition, but did not give up. He worked at different places and returned to Surajgarh with a vision of social development of Surajgarh. In the pursuit, he contributed towards education and women empowerment relentlessly.

Openess: Headmaster ji was open to new ideas, if he found merit in them. Be it educating his daughter and daughter-in-laws in the times of Purdah System or using English as the medium of instruction. In small village like Surajgarh, where people were reluctant to study, he realized the need of English as the language for masses to fight the British system. He initiated NCC and Social responsibility camps in PB high School.

Conviction: He had strong conviction about education, Social Reforms and women empowerment. He worked relentlessly in these areas. He facilitated the education of needy by arranging for the scholarship or depositing their fees on his own. He helped his pupil to pursue their education, despite their financial weakness.

Communication: He was a good communicator. He had a good hold on verbal as well as written communication. He was a strong orator. People still remember his speeches as the teacher at Chirawa High School and as headmaster at PB High School.

Organizer: Headmaster ji initiated School Newsletter at PB High School. He himself took initiative to organize NCC for the students and would even accompany the students, if they had to go out of town for the camps.

Strategic Planner: Headmaster ji had ability to think about opportunities of tomorrow and had ability to look forward. He had envisioned PB High School as an English Medium school, which has turned true. He would even counsel his students to face the hardships of present to fetch the better results in the future and today many of his students feel indebted as headmasterji's guidance helped them pave a comfortable & better life.

Idealistic: Headmaster ji was idealistic and always lead by example. He would do whatever he wanted others to do. He was man of high self -esteem. He would even argue with the Trustees of the school, if he would not agree to their viewpoint, due to which trustees, held him in high esteem.

Love for friends

Banwarilal Dungarka would ask him to show his muffler and if he liked it, he would give this away to his friend.

Teach his children

Teach his children and would focus on Studies.

Self- Respect

Despite the fact that everybody wanted employment at Birla's and hence would always be sycophants of Birlas. But Rambilas ji, himself never approached anybody to seek favour for the job. He always said, "Your work is counted and not your flattery."

A very Patient teacher

Rambilas ji had a lot of patience. He believed that, "A teacher should never hit the disciplines to make them study. The awe and reverence towards the teacher should be enough for the disciple to mobilize their efforts towards studies." Rambilas ji always followed this. His disciples narrated, "Headmaster ji would never mind repeating the explanation, any number of times, till the student would not be clear."

Head master ji – A good human being

At the time of crop cutting and storing, he would himself go to the farm and took the tasks. Sultan Singh, his sons, other youth from Raghunathpur, would go to his farm and would take the charge of the crop cutting, chaffing and storing. Dulichand ji reimences," Headmaster ji would bring food of 25 people to the farm, which would have sweets also. And would then feed everybody working on the farm. In those days that kind of food was hard to get."

Pitra Paksh Ekadashi and Rambilas ji's love for his forefathers

The male progeny of Rambilas ji's clan expired on Ekadashi and hence, shradha tarpan of all males was done on Ekadashi during the Pitra Paksh.

On Shradh paksh Ekadashi, he would feed 100-150 people with Kheer-Puri, to satiate his ancestors.

Madan lal ji Pushkarna remembers and narrates, "On this day, Rambilas ji would instruct his family to prepare kheer of 50 kg Milk, Pudi, jalebi and Sabzi. He would invite all his relatives and friends for the feast. He would personally come to me, to invite me for the lunch and would insist that, if I would not come, he would not take lunch. This was the affection he had."

Chapter 17

Rambilas Sharma - Educational leadership exemplified

Points covered

- **Rambilas Sharma as an educational leader for rural development and overall development**
- **Courage**
- **Respect for profession**
- **Empowerment**
- **Deep Commitment**
- **A sense of purpose**
- **Justice**
- **Temperance**

Chapter 17

Rambilas Sharma - Educational leadership exemplified

Rambilas ji had all the traits of educational Leader. He was consistent and had high expectation from his students. He was very ambitious about the success of his pupil. He consistently demonstrated that disadvantage need not be the barrier to achievement and hence he provided financial assistance to the students who did not had money to continue their education. He would even provide lodging and food to his students from the near by villages & that too free of cost. He would take personal care of the staff members and would inquire about their needs.

He was expert at assessment & the tracking of pupil progress with appropriate support and intervention based on the detailed knowledge of individual student. He was highly inclusive, having complete regard for the progress and personal development of every student.

He not only helped his students in the class room but outside the classroom. He developed a rapport with their parents and also with the community to support learning and progress of the students.

He identified with and contributed to the community of teachers, learners and leaders and influences others towards improved educational practice. He was dynamic, reflective and constantly evolving.

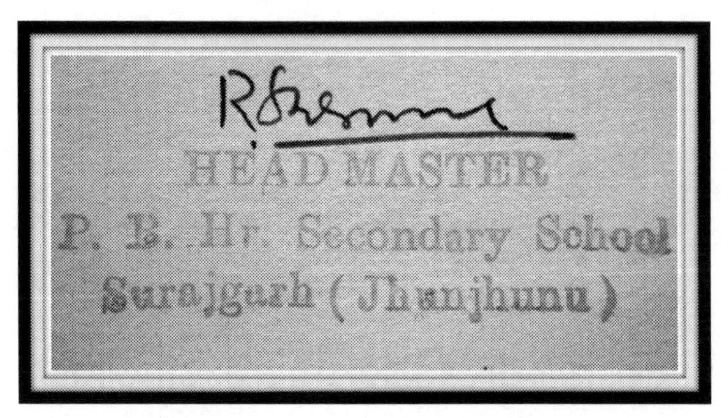

Picture Reference 53: Signature of Heaadmasterji

Dr. Larry Lezotte was one of the pioneers of the Effective Schools movement, which began in 1966 in response to a controversial report written by sociologist James Coleman. Coleman's report stated that schools could do little to support students' academic achievement, because achievement was predominantly related to the demographics and socioeconomic class of the surrounding community. Headsmasterji has believed and practiced the same in his educational professional carreer.

Lezotte's Effective Schools research, articulated in his 2010 book *What Effective Schools Do*, aimed to prove that schools could have a significant positive impact on their students' achievement regardless of other circumstances. At its heart, Lezotte's research stressed the seven "Correlates of Effective Schools." These factors were characteristics of effective schools across the racial and socioeconomic spectrum. To be an effective school, a school must:

Be a Safe and Organized Place

An effective school must first be a place where students can feel safe, physically and emotionally. It must be a supportive community where kids—and teachers—of all backgrounds can focus on learning. To create a climate of safety, halls and classrooms must be free of behavior like fighting, bullying, and harassment. That said, a safe environment is not created merely through punishment.

A 2011 study by Michael Thompson, researcher and director of the Justice Center at the Council of State Governments, shows that suspension and expulsion as discipline for "discretionary violations" actually do more harm than good for the individual student. They also damage the sense of community within the school. Students who receive suspensions and expulsions for discretionary violations are three times more likely to end up in a juvenile detention center the following year, and an authoritarian system creates an oppressive atmosphere where learning and school effectiveness are impaired.

To achieve a safe environment where kids are free to reach their potential academically, Thompson advocates for schools to focus on preventing misbehavior by implementing school-wide "positive behavior interventions." According to Thompson, these interventions should stress social skills and emotional learning, to teach students conflict resolution and cultural understanding.

Lezotte advocates similar methods of positivity. According to Lezotte, teachers, parents, and other mentors need to encourage a learning environment in school-age kids by treating schools as "sacred places." How society values school as a whole culture has everything to do with how students will engage with their own education. When students regard school as an institution with higher respect, they will enter the school with attitudes more conducive to learning, Lezotte says.

Headmaster ji believed that the students require guidance and counseling and not sheer punishment. He mentored his disciples not only with respect to their studies but also in other walks of life like carreer.

Set High Expectations for Students

Effective schools expect students to succeed. Because of that, students at these schools learn more. Psychology researcher Robert Rosenthal conducted an experiment in the 1960s where teachers were given a class of randomly selected students, and were told that these students' IQ test scores indicated that they had a high potential for growth that school year. When they took the IQ test again at the end of the year, the results showed that "the kids actually got smarter when they were expected to get smarter by their teachers," says Rosenthal. Students in classes where the researchers didn't plant these expectations did not show the same dramatic improvement. This happened because teachers gave more praise, remedial instruction, and opportunity for classroom participation to the students who were perceived as more capable. Students in turn found the lessons more interesting and approachable.

Teachers at effective schools genuinely believe that every kid has the raw materials to be a successful student, according to Lezotte's research. In a practical sense, this means that effective teachers make a conscious effort to give equal opportunity for all students to respond during class, provide thoughtful feedback to every student, and are willing to re-teach concepts that students have not mastered.

> ***Headmaster ji would teach and reteach the concepts till they were clear to his students. One of his students mentioned, "We could ask him the question, as many times as we wanted and he (Headmasterji) would not even frown"***

Have a Relatable Leader

In an effective school, the principal is a "leader of leaders." He or she is not just an authority figure, but also a "coach, partner, and cheerleader," says Lezotte. A leader of leaders does not operate in a top-down authority structure, but realizes that the best solutions come from a collaborative effort.

According to Lezotte, to show the kind of leadership that inspires and creates an enriching community in the school, the principal must be visible. She must be accessible not only to teachers but also to the student body—walking the halls, cheering at games, and supporting extra-curricular events. It is also the principal's responsibility to assess data about school effectiveness and implement strategies to address areas that need improvement.

Principal Robert Mastruzzi from John F. Kennedy High School in the Bronx, New York, was an example of a principal who motivated staff and students to achieve their potential, writes Sara Lawrence in her 1983 book *The Good High School.* While teachers praised his contagious energy and students were comfortable around him because of his warm personality, these weren't the only reasons he was a great leader. Mastruzzi's greatest strength was his vision for the school. His passionate belief that the students "are all winners" fueled his educational philosophy. "Each year I tell the faculty to increase their expectations of students. You ask for more and you get more," Mastruzzi says. Lawrence writes that his willingness to innovate was moderated by a sense for what wasn't working, and he met challenges by listening to his colleagues' perspectives before making changes.

> ***Headmasterji had a vision for school. He wanted his students to have all round development and hence, he started NCC at PB High School and convinced the parents of the students to allow their wards to go for NCC camps. He also encouraged students to participate in different sports & tournaments.***

State a Clear Mission

"Vision animates, inspires, transforms purpose into action," says Warren Bennis, a pioneer in the field of leadership studies. An effective principal must uphold a vision for the school and clearly articulate it to so teachers, administration, and parents can be united in striving for higher achievement.

In *What Effective Schools Do*, Lezotte points to principals' vague goals or interest in maintaining the status quo as common pitfalls of less effective schools. He says administrations are often unwilling to dedicate the resources and effort it takes to follow through on vision-driven change.

An effective mission emphasizes innovation and improvement in providing learning for all—students and educators of all backgrounds. The principal can make a mission effective by being persistent and energetic in sharing her vision with faculty, students, and parents to unite their goals. All of these members of the community must commit to this mission and take responsibility for its impact on the curriculum and learning environment.

Teachers especially should translate this mission so that it's pertinent to how they teach their classes, Lezotte writes. When the curriculum is designed with the mission in mind, it becomes easier to identify gaps in students' education and address the deficiencies. The school begins operating as one effective organism instead of a loose network of individuals with their own agendas. The mission becomes an ideal that guides everyone's efforts on a daily basis.

Headmaster ji was a role model for his colleagues. He insisted on maintain the session plans for the courses they taught in that academic year. They would also take note of the assignments given to the students.

METHOD OF TEACHING 9

Instead of extracts from Text Books on Method of Teaching, a brief statement in your own words of how the subject is taught may be written below.

...glish VII to X

Before the commencement of the lesson some introductory questions are asked on the previous lesson. If the lesson is a continuous one some revisional questions will be asked and they will serve as a preparation for the new lesson.

If the lesson is a long one it will be divided into units. Each unit will be taken separately. First of all model reading by the teacher will be given on the first unit. Sometimes silent reading of will be done by pupils provided that the passage is an easy one. Only five or six minutes will be given for this purpose.

When the reading is over the difficult words and phrases will be explained to the class by means of teaching aids. Grammatical points occurring in the text will be dealt with.

After finishing the difficulty of words and phrases individual reading will be undertaken. It will be conducted by four or five students selected from among the students. Firstly the intelligent readers will be asked to read the passage one by one while the weaker ones will simply be active listeners. When they have finished it some of the weaker boys will be called upon to read the passage. Thus they will improve the reading.

In the end some recapitulatory questions will be asked in order to test the boys whether they have grasped the substance of the lesson explained by the teacher.

Picture reference 54: Hand written notes from teacher's diary of Rambilas Sharma-1965

VIII

LIST OF HOLIDAYS* TO BE OBSERVED DURING THE SESSION 196 -6 .

Serial No.	Name of holiday	Date	Days	No. of days
१	बरावफ़ात	१२-७-६५	सोमवार	१
२	स्वतंत्रता दिवस	१५-८-६५	रविवार	१
३	रक्षा बन्धन	१२-८-६५	बृहस्पतिवार	१
४	जन्माष्टमी	१९-८-६५	बृहस्पतिवार	१
५	गांधी जयन्ती	२-१०-६५	शनिवार	१
६	दशहरा	३-४-५ अक्टूबर	रविवार से मंगलवार	३
७	गुरुनानक दिवस	९-११-६५	मंगलवार	१
८	शीतकालीन अवकाश	२५ से ३१ दिसम्बर	शनिवार से शुक्रवार	७
९	दीपमालिका	१५ से २८ अक्टूबर	रविवार से बृहस्पतिवार	१२
१०	गणतंत्र दिवस	२६ जनवरी	बुधवार	१
११	शिवरात्रि	१८-२-६६	शुक्रवार	१
१२	होली	६-७-८ मार्च	रविवार से मंगलवार	३
१३	ईदुल फ़ितर			
१४	रामनवमी	३० मार्च	बुधवार	१
१५	महावीर जयन्ती	३-४-६५	रविवार	१
१६	ईदुलजुहा			१
१७	मोहर्रम			१
	बरावफात	१२-७-६५		
	स्वतंत्रता दिवस	१५-८-६५		
	जन्माष्टमी	१९-८-६५		
	शिक्षक दिवस	५-९-६५		
	गांधी जयन्ती	२-१०-६५		
	संयुक्त राष्ट्र दिवस	२४-१०-६५		
	गुरुनानक जयन्ती	८-११-६५		
	बाल दिवस	१४-११-६५		
	ईसा जन्म दिवस	२५-१२-६५		
	गणतंत्र दिवस	२६-१-६६		
	बसन्त पंचमी			
	दयानन्द दिवस	२-३-६६		
	रामनवमी	३०-३-६६		
	महावीर जयन्ती	३-४-६६		
	बुद्ध पूर्णिमा	५-५-६६		

*All holidays to be observed in your Institution together with their dates and days may be filled in by you.

Picture reference 55: From teachers diary of Headmasterji year 1965-66

Monitor Students' Progress

Lezotte's research into the values of effective schools found that students who were regularly tested on their academic progress were more successful than those who weren't. Frequent teacher-written evaluations give teachers the information they needed to make changes if some or all students weren't mastering class material.

While effective schools use assessments, Lezotte believes teachers can and should assess the students' learning more holistically and less formally than standardized exams—relying less on multiple-choice tests and giving more attention to portfolios and presentations. Students should also be encouraged to monitor themselves by keeping progress charts and revisiting graded assignments.

> ***Headmaster ji believed in continuous evaluation of his students. He would not wait for the final examinations to give feedback to the students, rather would continuously give feedback to the students, so that they can improvise & develop. He maintained the records of the different evaluative components.***

Provide the Opportunity to Learn

Students tend to learn the things they spend the most time on. Teachers at effective schools are aware of limited instruction time and create a syllabus with that in mind. Keeping the mission at the forefront, teachers must create a syllabus that allows for not just all material to be covered, but also for it to be mastered, within the time constraints of the class. The syllabus must be flexible enough to allow re-teaching when the students are having trouble with certain key concepts.

In effective schools, teachers must sometimes practice "organized abandonment" when approaching their lesson plans. If students aren't mastering fundamental skills like reading, then teachers and schools may have to abandon lower-priority learning experiences until students are caught up to the appropriate standards. While organized abandonment is essential for true learning in limited timeframes, Lezotte and others advocate for more time spent in school in general, starting that schools could be more effective with shorter vacations and longer school days.

> ***Headmaster ji prepared the lesson plans and kept the record of the same. He would review this lesson plan every year and incorporate the new points to bridge the gap, if it exists.***

Build a True Partnership Between Home and School

The most effective schools have what Lezotte calls an authentic partnership with parents. At the most basic level, Lezotte says, teachers and staff must be able to rely on parents to get their children to school on time and regularly, and parents must be assured "that their children are entering a safe and caring place."

But a true home and school partnership goes much further. Teachers and parents work together to help kids get the most out of their assignments. Parents devote time to tutor their children, and teachers provide clear directions for how parents can help in a productive way. This strategy is most effective when teachers and parents have an open line of communication and can share notes on the student's progress.

According to Lezotte, effective schools go beyond purely academic matters when it comes to bridging home and school. In the most effective relationship between home and school, parents and other community agencies work together to address problems that are not uniquely school-based, says Lezotte. Drug use, bullying, and gang activity "are all serious problems where the school can contribute to the solution, but the school can't solve them alone." In an ideal situation, the community as a whole works as a team to tackle these issues and creates a better environment for learning, and a better society.

Headmasterji had a good rapport with his students as well as their family. He would know about the family of all his students. This gave him insight to identify the socio-economic background of these kids and hence, understand them better and also guide them accordingly. He would pay the fees of the student, who came from humble background.

Chapter 18

Rambilas ji's Psychometric Analysis for understanding his personality

Points covered

- **Understanding Personality**
- **Daily Routine**
- **Different influence on his personality**
- **Likes & Dislikes**
- **Food Habits**
- **Clothing**
- **Charismatic Aura**
- **Spell bounding speech**
- **Language command**
- **Belief system**

Chapter 18

Rambilas ji's Psychometric Analysis for understanding his personality

Psychometrics is the field of study concerned with the theory and technique of psychological measurement. One part of the field is concerned with the objective measurement of skills and knowledge, abilities, attitudes, personality traits, and educational achievement.

Big five traits or Five Factor Model (FFM) or NEO-PI scale, is a scale for the psychometric testing. It analyses the personality of an individual on five traits, Openess to Experience, Conscientiousness, Extraversion, Agreeableness and Neuroticism.

- **Openness to experience**: (*inventive/curious* vs. *consistent/cautious*). Appreciation for art, emotion, adventure, unusual ideas, curiosity, and variety of experience. Openness reflects the degree of intellectual curiosity, creativity and a preference for novelty and variety a person has. It is also described as the extent to which a person is imaginative or independent, and depicts a personal preference for a variety of activities over a strict routine. Some disagreement remains about how to interpret the openness factor, which is sometimes called "intellect" rather than openness to experience.

  Rambilas ji was high on the "Openess to experience" scale. He was curious to learn new things. He earned many educational degrees which were as varied as degree in Sanskrit and also degree in English.

- **Conscientiousness**: (*efficient/organized* vs. *easy-going/careless*). A tendency to be organized and dependable, show self-discipline, act dutifully, aim for achievement, and prefer planned rather than spontaneous behaviour.

  Rambilasji was self- disciplined and organized. He maintained the dairies of his teaching sessions very distinctively. He kept proper records of all his assignments. His self-discipline was exemplary. He was very punctual and dutiful. The school management trusted him and considered him dependable.

- **Extraversion**: (*outgoing/energetic* vs. *solitary/reserved*). Energy, positive emotions, surgency, assertiveness, sociability and the tendency to seek stimulation in the company of others, and talkativeness.

  Rambilasji was neither high on extraversion nor high on introversion. He was an ambivert, as although he was not garrulous but he was assertive. He would stand up for the cause, for example he advocated women education. He would communicate his views to the concerned.

- **Agreeableness**: (*friendly/compassionate* vs. *analytical/detached*). A tendency to be compassionate and cooperative rather than suspicious and antagonistic towards others. It is also a measure of one's trusting and helpful nature, and whether a person is generally well tempered or not.

  Rambilasji was moderate on agreeableness. He was cooperative and would help others. But he was not docile and had his own point of view, which he would definitely put forward, if he did not agree to them.

- **Neuroticism**: (*sensitive/nervous* vs. *secure/confident*). The tendency to experience unpleasant emotions easily, such as anger, anxiety, depression, and vulnerability. Neuroticism also refers to the degree of emotional stability and impulse control and is sometimes referred to by its low pole, "emotional stability".

Rambilasji was very balanced in his demeanour. He was emotionally stable. Despite the post-retirement phase with lows, he always shows a stable and balanced behaviour. Failures never stopped him to explore further.

Besides, FFM model, few other psychological traits like self- esteem, self -monitoring and needs are considered.

Self-esteem- Self-esteem is how we value ourselves; it is how we perceive our value to the world and how valuable we think we are to others. Self-esteem affects our trust in others, our relationships, our work – nearly every part of our lives. Positive self-esteem gives us the strength and flexibility to take charge of our lives and grow from our mistakes without the fear of rejection.

Rambilasji hadpositive self- esteem. He was confident and knew his strengths and weaknesses. He had no fear of rejection and would learn from his mistakes.

Self -monitoring- Self-monitoring is defined as a personality trait that refers to an ability to regulate behaviour to accommodate social situations. People who closely monitor themselves are categorized as high self-monitors and often behave in a manner that is highly responsive to social cues and their situational context.

Rambilasji was high self -monitor. Since his childhood, he stayed away from his house for education and then his early career. But he could adjust in any situation that he stayed. He could accommodate himself as per the social requirements.

Different needs of an individual as identified by Mc Cleland's

Need for Achievement

People motivated by achievement, need challenging, but not impossible, projects. They thrive on overcoming difficult problems or situations. People motivated by achievement, work very effectively either alone or with other high achievers.

Rambilas ji was high on Need for achievement which is evident from the decks of qualifications that he earned. He always wanted to achieve higher and higher. This need was **Highest** among all the three needs.

Affiliation

People motivated by affiliation work best in a group environment, so try to integrate them with a team (versus working alone) whenever possible. They also don't like uncertainty and risk. These people often don't want to stand out, so they want to be praised in private rather than in front of others.

Rambilas ji's need for affiliation was moderate. He had desire to build rapport with people but was not always obsessed with team work.

Power

Those with a high need for power work best when they're in charge. Because they enjoy competition, they do well with goal-oriented projects or tasks. They may also be very effective in negotiations or in situations in which another party must be convinced of an idea or goal.

Although Rambilasji, liked to take up goal-oriented projects but the position power never allured him, to the extent that at one point in his career, he worked under Principal Shri Ram Pratap ji, who was less qualified than him, but he never had any grudge.

Rambilas ji's persona can be summarized as one who possessed enormous energy. He was successful planner. There was sudden occurrence of incidents in his life. He was intelligent and was successful in any profession that he pursued. He preferred to work independently. His students developed and reached political positions. He took part in innovative and creative activity.

Headmaster ji always had his own opinion and acted as per his own judgement. He was highly determined. He had strong will power and was bold and diligent. He earned name and fame in the society. He constantly worked on new ideas in his field of work.

He was indifferent to money & materialistic things. Infact, he also suffered financial losses, when he ventured into bangle business. He had sudden ups & Downs in his life. He was practical &well organized.

Picture Reference 56: Headmasterji

Daily Routine: start day with worshipping sun god, believed in power of gayatri, getting out after having food at home, and return home in evening.

Different influence on his personality

Likes:

Dislikes

Food habbits: sangria ki sabji, kheer, roti,

Clothings: perfect dressed, like tie and suit, Jodhpuri suit

Charismatic Aura

Spell bounding speech: in hindi, English and urdu

Language command: good command over English, hindi, Sanskrit and urdu.

Personality: simplicity in living –non smoker, non-drinker, tea totaller, 100% veg.

Inspirations of life: Vivekanandji, Sadar patel

Headmasterji's love in life was reading

Headmasterji's belief systems: non political, social and educational development of society at par.

Chapter 19

Life in post retirement era, illness and last journey (year 1972-1977)

Points covered

- Retired from PB high School in 1971
- But mission for education continued…
- Joined school at jhunjhunu.
- Appointed Rajendra Sharma…
- Story from raju Sharma.
- Life at PC college, Mathura
- Joining at Farah, Mathura
- Good life at vraj bhoomi
- Premsukh das oil mills management and rambilasji.
- Rambilasji Sharma as director of the college.
- Life at Ballabhgarh
- Secretary / Managing trustee at ballabhgarh "agarwal college"
- Marriage of Sajjankumar and Sunitikumar.
- Extending vacations
- Illness-kidney problem, 1977.
- Both kidney failure.
- Admitting in Jaipur Hospital.
- The pain in life.
- The visitors in surajgarh in last time.
- Omprakash and the gayatrimantra.
- Adhytmik punji of the puja and the gayatrimantra.
- Foreseen the death.
- Instructing all family members.
- Asking wife not to fast on that day.
- Died on: 07-11 1977.

Chapter 19

Life in post retirement era, illness and last journey (year 1972-1977)

1971- School at Ishwarpura

Immediately after retiring from PB High School in 1971, Rambilas ji joined Seth Ishwardas Tekriwal madhyamik vidyalaya at Ishwarpura, Jhunjhunu district. Ishwarpura village was around 20 miles from Jhunjhunu. It was not possible to commute everyday between Jhunjhunu and Ishwarpura, at the age of 58 years. Moreover the water of the wells at Ishwarpura had hard and salty water. Headmasterji stayed at Ishwardasji's Dharamshaala at Ishwarpura only. Since, the proper water and food was not available in Ishwarpura, the in-laws of Rambilasji's son Sh Savita Prakash ji, used to send food and water every day for Rambilas ji through an employee of the same school, who commuted every day from Jhunjhunu to Ishwarpura. Headmaster ji appointed Sh. Rajendra Sharma in the same school, who worked there for six months. Later Rajendra ji got the opportunity as a clerk in the government school, but the requirement of the job was two years work experience. Rajendra ji reminisces, "When I got this offer, I was into fix. Although I have worked for more than two years but had no experience certificate, as I worked on the daily basis. Ishwarpura job was my first job as the full time employee which was only for six months. I was not sure and discussed this matter with headmaster ji. Knowing my earlier work experience, he had been kind enough to give me the certificate of two years of work experience. This changed my life and I lead my life comfortably. I retired in the year 2012, and because of his support, I am a pensioner and am secured. I owe this to Headmasterji."

Rambilas ji at Farah, Mathura 1972

Rambilas ji joined Seth Premsukhdas College at Farah as Director in 1972. His distant cousin, Basudev ji Sharma worked at Bansidhar Premsukhdas oil mills, Agra. Once headmasterji visited Agra and met Basudevji. Since, the college he worked with and the oil mill had same management, headmasterji also happened to meet the chairman of the management. When the Chairman met him, he offered him to also look into the affairs of oil mill. When Basudev ji heard this, he was worried and he said to headmasterji, "You are so educated and learned. Your presence at mill, might affect my position here. It would be difficult for me. Please don't accept this proposal." On listening to this, Rambilasji decided not only to reject this proposal but also to resign from the college."

Rambilas ji at Vallabhgarh 1974

After that from 1974 to 1975 he worked at Agrawala High School, Vallabhgarh as Director and later on was promoted as Managing trustee. Narendra Singh Gupta was the trustee of the school and he and his family respected Headmasterji as fatherly figure. Headmaster ji had instrumental role in development of the school. He hired well educated teachers and even started English medium education. Today this school has expanded into a college also.

The wedding of his sons Sh. Sajjan and Suniti Kumar was planned in June 1975 and hence, Headmaster ji went to Surajgarh. He extended his leaves after the wedding, as he was not well.

He returned to Vallabhgarh, after some time, to resume his duties. But his health by then, had become a major reason of concern and very often he would be unwell. So, his mother asked him to come back to Surajgarh.

Return to Surajgarh- 1976

Rambilas ji returned to Surajgarh in 1976. The family members were concerned about his health. They took him to different doctors and finally he was diagnosed with kidney problem. So, he was referred for treatment to Jaipur, which was the only nearby city with the sophisticated hospital. He was admitted to the hospital in Jaipur. The doctors diagnosed him with renal failure. In those days, kidney transplantation in India was in its infancy and was also not a sure success. So, Rambilas ji decided not to go for renal transplantation and requested his sons to take him back to Surajgarh. All the sons were anxious and were disheartened with this. Since, his eldest son, Om Prakash ji was already settled in Jaipur; he requested headmasterji to stay with him for few days. One day anxious Om Prakash ji, asked his father, "What would I do, if something happens to you?" Hearing that, Headmasterji said, "You are 41 years old right now. When my father passed away, I was only 37. If I could manage life after my father, you would definitely be able to manage it. Life teaches everything and way of living to everybody. So you need not to worry." Next day, he requested OmPrakash ji to take him back to Surajgarh.

Rambilasji's Mahaprayan

After reaching back to Surajgarh, his friends and relatives would come to meet him. But Headmasterji was in great pain. He would writhe in pain and people could hear him in pain even at half a kilometre from his place. He could not bear this pain and one day called Om Prakash ji and asked him, "Can you give me something?" Om Prakash ji was stunned and he said, "What do I have that, I can give you? I am nobody, as compared to you. You have reached heights in every field. Still, if I have anything that you ask for, I would definitely give you." On that Headmasterji said, "You have been a great devotee of Maa Gayatri and have completed thousands of rosaries. I cannot bear the pain anymore. Could you please, give me the mahatmaya and his spirituality of all your Gayatri mantra to me? So that, I can die calmly." OmPrakash ji immediately brought the copper Lota full of water and gave his father all his Mahatmaya and Spirituality. After that Headmasterji was little relaxed. Next day was Ekadashi and Janki devi, wife of headmasterji, fasted on ekadashi. But headmasterji told his wife not to fast on that day. On Ekadashi, 7th November 1977, Janki devi went to temple and when she was in the temple, she heard the news of the Headmasterji mahaprayana.

Chapter 20

Rambilas ji's children

Points covered

- **Omprakash ji**
- **Satya Prakash ji**
- **Gayatri devi**
- **Savita Prakash ji**
- **Sajjan Kumar ji**
- **Suniti Kumar ji**

Chapter 20

Rambilas ji's children

Rambilas ji had six children: five sons and a daughter. He made sure that all his kids took proper education. His belief in education facilitated smooth life journey of his children.

1. **OmPrakash ji:** OmPrakash ji is the eldest son of Rambilas ji. He was born in 1936. He completed his education and got government job and became gazetted officer. He married Durga devi, daughter of Kesar Deo ji, of Dheendhwa wala clan. He had three sons and a daughter- Late Sushil Kumar, Late Ashok Kumar and Rajesh Kumar and daughter Beena. The family is settled in Mahapura, Jaipur, Rajasthan.
2. **Satya Prakash Ji:** Satya Prakash ji is the second son of Rambilas ji. He was born in 1938. He completed his education and got government job. He married Gita Devi, daughter of Sh. Birbal ji, of Morwa wala clan. He has a son and two daughters- Shashi, Dinesh, Vandana. The family is settled in Jaipur, Rajasthan.
3. **Gayatri Devi:** Gayatri devi is the only daughter of Rambilas ji. She was born in 1944. She completed her education and passed Vidya Vinodini exam. She married Vishwanathji, son of Sh.Brij Lal ji Dhandh, of Pilani. She has three sons and three daughters- Shashi, Anita, Shalu, Prem Prakash, Ravi Prakash and Rahul. The family is settled in Pilani, Rajasthan.
4. **Savita Prakash Ji:** Savita Prakash ji is the third son of Rambilas ji. He was born in 1946. He completed his education and did diploma in engineering. He chose to work in private organizations like HMT, Ajmer; Birla Mills, Bombay; Hindustan Copper, Khetri. He took

the projects abroad like Bangladesh and UAE. He then started his own enterprise "RJ Industries." He married Sita Devi, daughter of Sh. Keshar Deo ji, of Jhunjhunu. Sita Devi is well educated and has earned B.Ed degree. Savita Prakash ji has two sons and a daughter- Sandeep, Sanjeev and Seema. The family is settled in Ahmedabad, Gujarat.

Picture Reference 57: 1971- Headmasterji with his son-SavitaPrakash in the later's wedding

5. **Sajjan Kumar Ji:** Sajjan Kumar ji is the fourth son of Rambilas ji. He was born in 1952. He completed his education and got government job. He married Hemlata devi, daughter of Sh.Satya dev Mishra, of Bagad. He has a son and two daughters- Kuldeep, Mahima and Manisha. The family is settled in Jaipur, Rajasthan.
6. **Suniti Kumar ji:** Suniti Kumar ji is the fifth son of Rambilas ji. He was born in 1954. He completed his education and got government

job as teacher. He married Santosh devi, daughter of Sh.Ramesh Kumar Haritwal, of Chirawa. He has two sons- Deepak and Rishabh. The family is settled in Churu, Rajasthan.

Year 1971: SAVITAPRAKSH(HEADMASTERJI'S MARRIAGE)

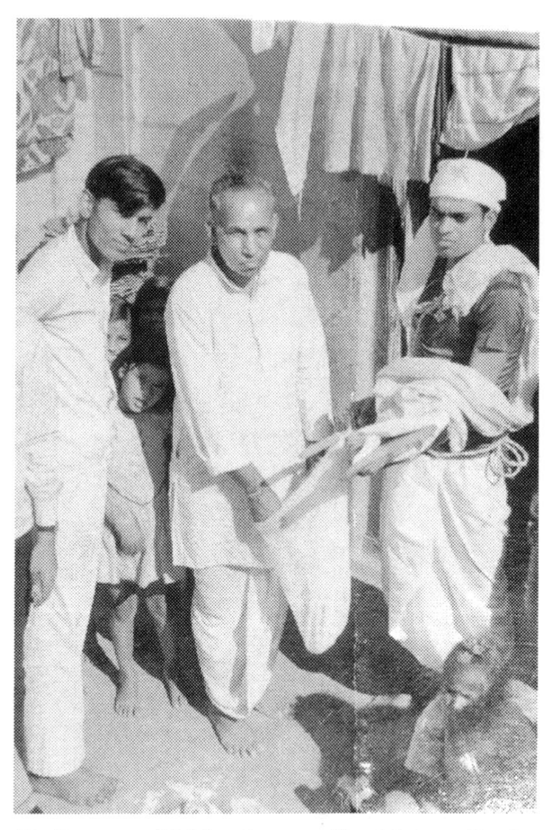

Picture Reference 58:Headmasterji with son Savitaprakash and other kids of family during a ceremony at Surajgarh(early 1971)

Picture Reference 59: Headmasterji in white in centre with famous industrialist Hariram Tibrewal(in black suit), with cabinet minister-Seshram Ola(behind Hariram tibrewal 's head), in the photo are also seen headmasterjis son Omprakash, Satyaprakash, Sajjan and others.

Picture Reference 60: Year 1971-marriage party of son-Savitaprakash, Headmasterji in pure white kurta –right sitting

Picture Reference 61: year 1971-marriage of son-Savitaprakash (in black suit with turban riding horse), Headmasterji in pure white kurta.

Chapter 21

Educational vision of Headmasterji for Surajgarh lives beyond his life

Points covered

- **Life after death of Headmasterji**
- **Family destroyed all the documents related to him**
- **Condition of the wife after Headmasterji**
- **Headmasterji's mother died in 1979**
- **The education mission of Headmasterji still continues after his death**
- **Start of first PG college in Surajgarh**
- **Start of first Engineering college in Surajgarh**
- **The mission of the English School and teaching**
- **Year 2013- Idea of writing about Headmasterji on his 100th Birthday and the grandson Sandeep Sharma**
- **Ideas about memories and book**

Chapter 21

Educational vision of Headmasterji for Surajgarh lives beyond his life

Headmasterji died in the year 1977. By then all his children were married and settled in their profession. Since his mother was alive then, headmasterji's wife decided to stay back in Surajgarh to look after her mother-in-law as that was headmasterji's desire. But his mother did not survive for many years after headmasterji's death and passed away after two years in 1979. Janki Devi, headmasterji's wife, who was asthama patient, also did not survive for quite long and bid adieu to this world in 1980.

After death of Janki Devi, the ancestral house was looked after by Sajjan Kumar ji's family as Sajjan Kumar ji had his job in Surajgarh. Rest of the other sons, worked at different places in different cities of India and hence made the respective cities, the place of their residence.

In Surajgarh Headmasterji's family still owns, a house, 25 Bigha farm, a Nohra and a baada and have remained attached to the roots.

Savitaprakashji has taken life time membership of Surajgarh Brahaman Sabha and give donaton for the development of this association.

The education mission of Headmasterji still continues after his death.

Start of first PG college in Surajgarh.

The first pg college in surajgarh was started by one of the Headmasterji favourite student-Late. Jugal kishore barasia, in year 1984 after 7 yrs.

Start of first ENGG. College in Surajgarh.

Keystone group started en engineering college at pilod in surajgarhTehsil in year 2000.The Keystone Group of Institutions is promoted by a group of NRIs with vast technical and managerial expertise acquired through their education in top US colleges/universities and years of work experience in senior leadership roles and exposure in global corporate giants like American Express, Interpublic Group, JP Morgan Chase, Nokia Siemens.

The promoters after spending up to 14+ years in United States of America decided to return to their motherland and contribute to INDIA RISING at the grass roots level with a mission to transform the experience in higher education! To further this cause, the promoters formed a charitable trust back in July 2005 – Shree Kalka Devi Education Trust – a fitting tribute to the Goddess of time and change and the one seen as the Greatest Protector of all! The group then selected SURAJGARH – which literally translates into CASTLE OF THE RISING SUN – a location with fitting name to the vision of the group to establish a world class institution – Keystone Group of Institutions. The Keystone campus is a fully integrated residential one offering UG degrees in Engineering (B.Tech) and PG degree in Management (MBA) in the heart of the educational hub of the Shekhawati region near Pilani!

The mission of the English school and teaching for surajgarh was pioneer by Head masterji at PB High School in year 1950. Today there are 15 institutes connected to education and training.

4 schools, 1 government school, 2 coaching class, 7 computer institutes, 1 engineering college,

GOVT. SEC. SCHOOL, SURAJGARH Govt. School; GOVT. SEC. SCHOOL, SURAJGARH.

TIME LINE OF EVENTS	
Year	Event
1913	Birth Of Rambilas ji Sharma
1916	Initial Education in Sanskrit from Guruji & Grandfather Lokram ji Ghagshyan
1917	Started Schooling at Chirawa, Mahadeo Somany School
1922	Passed Fifth Board Exam at Chirawa Middle School
1927	Passed Tenth Standard Board Exam, Chirawa High School
1929	Passed Intermediate from MUIR central college, Allahabad, Affiliated to Agra University
1929	Got married to Janki Devi Choumal

1932	Passed BA(Hons) in English Literature
1932	First Graduate in the History Of Surajgarh
1933	Meeting with Thakur Raghubir Singh & joining of School of Bissau at Raghubir Singh's Request
1936	Passed MA(Hons) in English Literature from GC Lahore University
1936	Joined Chirawa Hogh School as a Teacher
1936	Birth of eldest Son, Om Prakash Ji
1938	Passed MA in Hindi from Agra University
1938	Came in contact with GD Birla at Chirawa High School
1942	Joined Birla High School, Okara, Lahore(Now Pakistan)
1943	Became Principal of Birla High School, Chirawa
1943	Birth of Second Son, Satya Prakash ji
1944	Joined Satluj Cotton mill, Okara
1944	KL Sehgal's Story
1945	Meeting Sardar Patel; Strike at Satluj Cotton Mill
1945	Birth Of only daughter Gayatri Devi
1946	Pre Partition Talks
1946	Sent family Back to Surajgarh
1946	Birth of Savita Prakash ji
1947	Came back to India along with Madan Lal ji Pushkarna
1947	GD Birla asked Headmaster ji to join Hind Motors
1948	Came in contact with Jay Dayal Dalmia and Ramkrishna Dalmia
1948	Joined as incharge at Dalmia concern at Guntoor, Andhra Pradesh. Company Now known as Meenakshi Chemicals Ltd
1949	Bhagwati's(Niece of Rambilasji) marriage
1949	Resigned from Dalmia's concern at Guntoor
1949	Started a venture of Bangle manufacturing
1950	Death of father, Gajanada ji
1950	Birth of Sajjan Kumar ji
1950	Joined PB High School
1952	First Election in Surajgarh
1953	Birth of Suniti Kumar ji

1954	Passed MA in Sanskrit from Allahabad University
1955	Principal of PB High School
1958	Visit of Vinoba Bhave at Surajgarh
1958	Marriage of OmPrakash Sharma
1959	PB High School won football trophy
1962	Marriage of Satya Prakash ji
1964	Member of Shri Krishna Parishad
1971	Retired from PB High School
1971	Marriage of Savita Prakash ji
1971	Joined as Principal at Ishwarpura School
1972	Birth Of Grandson Sandeep(Son of Savita Prakash ji)
1972	Joined Seth BP Inter college, Farah
1975	Marriage of Sajjan Kumar ji & also Suniti Kumar ji
1975	Joined Agarwal College, Vallabhgarh as Director
1976	Came Back to Surajgarh because ofailing Health
1976	Diagnosed with Kidney Problem
1977	Death Due to Kidney failure
1980	Death of mother, Harpyari Devi
1981	Death of Wife, Janaki Devi
2013	Idea struck to write a book on Headmasterji
2015	Book Published

Reference

- History of Rajasthan- by –James Todd
- Bhagirath Sharma, Kalabhawan photo studio, Surajgarh
- Paramhans pandit Ganesh narayan –bavalia baba –charitra sopan- by Sagarmal Sharma, published by sahitya mahavidhalaya chirawa. page no-56(sub header 43)
- Biography of GD birla by-Dariav Sharma, published from Delhi.
- Chirawa –atit se vartman- by Pt. Sagarmal Sharma, chirawa
- Shrikrishna parishad smaranika-silverjublee year, published in 1968.
- Biography of Murlidhar Dalmia- how to solve management problems- published by bhartiya vidhya bhavan, mumbai
- PROFILE OF BIRLA GROUPS OF COMPANIES64
- SHASTRI, DEVDUT (ED.) AAK BINDU: aak Sindhu, (Pryag)
- Sh.Jugal Kishore Birla, Samvat 2025.1968) p.114
- BUSINESS INDIA, (June 15-28, 1987), P.533.
- JAJU.R.N Maru Bhumi Ka Vaha Megh, (Hindi) (New Delhi: Raj paland sons), p.261.
- BUSINESS INDIA, (Dec, 24, 1990-JAN.6 1991) P.65
- COMMERCE, (New15, 1952), p.92
- TAKNET, D.K., Industrial Entrepreneurship of shekhwati
- Marwaris (Jaipur: Kumar Prakashan, 1987) p.120
- Ibid, p.121
- Ibid, p. 1229.
- CHENTSAL RAO, P B.M.Birla, his deeds and dreams, (New
- Delhi: 1985), p.2.
- Ibid, p.29.Ibid, p.30
- BUSINESS INDIA, (dec.24, 1990-jan.6, 1991), p.67
- BUSINESS INDIA, (dec.24.1990-jan.6.1991), p.67

- Ibid, p.67
- BUSINESS INDIA, (nov.16, 1990, -dec.9.1990) p.16
- INDIA TODAY, (Dec.24 1990.-Jan.6 1991), p.66
- BUSINESS INDIA, sep.16. -29, 1991), p.46
- Ibid, p.48
- **Rashtriya Balika madhaymik Vidhyalaya Surajgarh Smarika, 1983**
- http://www.Surajgarh.com. **Viewed on 26th October 2014**
- Vaidhya Chote lal ji Pranacharya Granth, Jhunjhunu Jila Vaidhya Sammalen.
- http://oldsettlersofsikkim.blogspot.in/2013/04/the-marwari-business-model.html
- http://www.neelimadalmiaadhar.com/blog/tag/dineshnandini-dalmia/
- etheses.saurashtrauniversity.edu/202/1/ajmera_bc_thesis_com.pdf
- Biography Of Hajarilal Sharma-Titled In Hindi- Yug Purush Hajarilal Sharma-Jivan Dirgha, Published From Chirawa.
- http://books.google.co.in/books?id=az6CAgAAQBAJ&pg=PA483&lpg=PA483&dq=the+strike+at+sutlej+cotton+mills+,+okara&source=bl&ots=yfSKkP6CQC&sig=tx2v_qpfZtLgNUS6nwX5wBVACn8&hl=en&sa=X&ei=Wy5jVMX0JtSOuATtmYH4DA#v=onepage&q=the%20strike%20at%20sutlej%20cotton%20mills%20%2C%20okara&f=false
- Usman Muhammad Khan, New Jersey 08054-3315 USA Wikimapia User: uzkmi Updated: August 30, 2012)
- http://www.shekhawati.in/history-of-shekhawati.